IN DEFENSE OF OUR CHILDREN

When Politics, Profit, and Education Collide

Elaine M. Garan, Ph. D.

D0836255

HEINEMANN
Portsmouth, NH

Heinemann
A division of Reed Elsevier Inc.
361 Hanover Street
Portsmouth, NH 03801–3912
www.heinemann.com

Offices and agents throughout the world

The author and publisher wish to thank those who have generously given permission to reprint borrowed material:

Figure 1: "Normal Bell-Shaped Curve" cartoon is used by permission of Roaring Lion E-book writer, author, and illustrator Georgia Hedrick.

Library of Congress Cataloging-in-Publication Data
Garan, Elaine M.
  In defense of our children : when politics, profit, and education collide / Elaine M. Garan.
    p.   cm.
  Includes bibliographical references and index.
  ISBN 0-325-00647-4 (alk. paper)
  1. Reading—United States.   2. Literacy programs—United States.
  I. Title.
  LB1050.2.G35   2004
  372.46'5—dc22   2003020700

Editor: Lois Bridges
Production: Elizabeth Valway
Cover design: Suzanne Heiser, Night & Day Design
Composition: Technologies 'N Typography, Inc.
Manufacturing: Steve Bernier

Printed in the United States of America on acid-free paper
08 07 06 05 04   ML   1 2 3 4 5

For my amazing little granddaughter,
Lilia Devi Baker Shakya

CONTENTS

Acknowledgments   vii

PART I: SCHOOL REFORM AND WHAT IT MEANS FOR OUR CHILDREN

Section I: Schools, Wizards, and Pulling Back Curtains   1

Dear Reader: Please Read This First   1

Introduction   2

Section II: Behind Curtain Number 1: School "Reform"   9

Scandal!   9

Asking the Right Questions   10

Beware of Buzzwords!   18

Behind the Curtain of No Child Left Behind   19

Section III: Behind the Curtain of Accountability: All About Testing   29

Testing 101   31

Why Many Children Must Be Left Behind by NCLB: How Standardized Tests Are Normed   43

Labeling Our Preschool Children   46

The Repercussions of Standardized Testing   50

Section IV: A Hard Look at Stress and Competition   56

Looking at Learning   66

PART II: WHAT IS LEARNING? HOW DO WE LEARN?

Section V: Bottom-Up Teaching, Methods, Materials, and Research   67

Skills-First, or Bottom-Up, View of Teaching/Learning   68

Section VI: Government-Approved Programs, Methods, and the Research Claims   81

Government-Approved Reading Programs   81

Scripted Manuals   82

More Intimidation   86

The Truth About the NRP Findings on Commercial
Reading Programs   89

Section VII: Top-Down Teaching, Methods, Materials, and Research   111

Reading Instruction: A Quick Overview of a
Top-Down Classroom   111

Back to the Reading Wars   121

The Need for Libraries   136

How Do Teaching Styles Affect Students'
Thinking and Behavior?   142

Back to the Beginning   145

Section VIII: What Can We Do About It?   147

References   152
Notes   159
Index   164

ACKNOWLEDGMENTS

There's a scene I just love in the movie *Sweet Dreams: The Patsy Cline Story* in which the whole ensemble's been on the road for a long, hard tour. They drag themselves onto the bus and collapse into their seats, too tired to even move. Then someone picks up a guitar and strums a few notes and then another person joins in and then another, and soon the whole group, who was too drained to even move a minute ago, is playing along. I love that scene because in it we see a group of people who are colleagues and friends and who keep each other going because their work is also their passion.

I am so lucky to be part of a ensemble like that. When one of us gets too tired or too discouraged and is ready to give up, someone else picks up that guitar and strums a note and before we know it, we're all up and at it again. Sometimes that person is Steve Krashen or Ardie Cole or Regie Routman, who all have a gift for bringing hope to teachers by celebrating a profession that is publicly maligned and insulted with relentless regularity these days. Often it's our mutual editor and friend, the remarkable Lois Bridges, who somehow manages to keep us all going when we're ready to give up.

I want to thank the teachers out there in the trenches, too, who struggle to maintain good practices against pressures from so many places that it's hard to even keep track of them all. Among those wonderful teachers are names that you may not know but who serve as an inspiration for me and for others, too, including Nancy Barth and Jenny Wilcock. And my gratitude goes to all the teachers who wrote to me after my last book was published. It seemed as if a letter always came along just when I needed it most.

Thanks also to the talented writers who have helped along the way, including Derek Boucher, Brett Dillingham, and Georgia Hedrick, who is not only a fine writer but a motorcycling ex-nun and a wickedly funny cartoonist to boot. I'm grateful also to Peter Duckett. Not only is his eye movement research an incredible contribution to the profession, but he was nice enough to walk me through it and answer my questions. I owe a lot to Alis

Headlam, too, for her insights into the brain research on dyslexia. Another researcher and teacher who helped me with the facts about Reading Recovery outcomes is my friend and colleague Judith Neal.

One of the indispensable behind-the-scenes unsung heroes at Heinemann is Elizabeth Valway, who meticulously cross-checked sources and helped me to clean up and clarify so much of the final manuscript.

I've relied a lot on Susan Ohanian's website as well as her work, and I'm indebted to her for providing these resources. Thanks also to that special group that guards the guards of politics and research. The members of this club to whom I'm indebted include Joanne Yatvin, who took a courageous first stand, Gerry Coles, Dick Allington, and of course, Steve Krashen. I'm glad they're on our side!

Last but not least, I want to thank my children, Holly Shakya and Chris Baker, for their suggestions and help in the writing. And as always, I'm grateful to my parents, Gene and Betty Garan. They're both still sending me news clippings about Florida schools, writing letters to the editor, and demanding accountability from our leaders. Both of my parents always stood up for what was right and they taught me to do the same. That is quite a gift. I have a lot to be grateful for.

Section I

SCHOOLS, WIZARDS, AND PULLING BACK CURTAINS

DEAR READER: PLEASE READ THIS FIRST

My son says that people don't read introductions to books. My daughter says that they do or they at least skim them. Whether you're a skipper or a skimmer, I hope you'll read this introductory section because it lays out the framework for what comes later on and I'll be referring to the ideas here throughout the book.

Whom Is This Book for and Why Am I Writing It?

After my last book was published, I received dozens of letters from teachers.[1] The message was almost always the same: Parents need to understand what's really happening in schools and so do journalists and legislators. They need to understand the truth about hot topics such as phonics, invented spelling, scripted reading programs, back-to-basics teaching methods, as well as high-stakes testing and accountability. And they need to understand what sweeping new school reforms mean for our children.

When I wrote this book, I imagined I was having a conversation with a friend. At many points in the book, I've included questions that teachers, parents, and students in teacher preparation classes can use for discussing the issues, the contrasting teaching methods, and the range of materials that are at the center of the debates over school reform. I hope this book can build a bridge between the home and the school and even the media, because our common goal is doing what's best for children.

1

INTRODUCTION

What Is a School?

I believe that many of us view public schools as a sort of sacred trust insulated from political pressures or financial exploitation. They are not, as you will see. What I want to help you discover and consider and *act* on is that schools are not just about learning facts or getting high scores on tests. As we will see, the teaching methods and materials used by schools, the way the school day is structured, and the underlying messages we communicate, often influence more than our children's academic performance. Those factors also impact our children's emotional development, their motivation, and how they feel about themselves.

It is these elusive, deeply personal characteristics that define us as individuals and determine our future success. Sometimes they are quite literally a matter of life and death. We learned this the hard way when "good students" and "quiet kids" came into their schools and killed their classmates and teachers. We know this too from the heartbreaking increase in teen suicides, school dropouts, and children who turn to gangs for a sense of belonging and self-worth.

Even though I had a college degree in teaching high school, I can still remember the nervousness I felt when I walked into my daughter's kindergarten classroom for my first parent-teacher conference. I had serious questions for the teacher about why my daughter was being forced to copy letters between hugely spaced lines even though she could already read and write messages and little stories in both capital and lowercase letters. Why, I wanted to ask, was she being forced into drills of alphabet learning that she had already mastered?

I sat there on one side of the teacher's desk while the teacher sat behind it. She had probably a dozen parents waiting for their turn to sit on the child's side of the desk to meet with her, and so I had maybe fifteen minutes to try to communicate what I wanted to say and to ask the questions I needed answers to.

Ultimately, I went against my best instincts and the best interests of my child and retaught her to form her letters in huge lines and forced her to copy instead of to continue creating messages and stories. I was intimidated by the school setting, and I gave into that intimidation. I did the same thing as a beginning teacher, too. I want to help you to do better than I did over the years.

The specifics changed, but the patterns of my reactions were repeated over and over again in one way or another for years over the course of my children's schooling. Looking back, I see that my intentions were always right and my instincts were mostly right. But the ways I approached situations—I'm embarrassed to say—were often either dead wrong or just not very effective at all.

Here are some of the mistakes I made: I was quiet or I let myself be silenced at the times I should have spoken up. I spoke up when I should have shut up. Sometimes I spoke up at the right time, but I did it in the wrong way and managed to antagonize the teacher or the principal. A good bit of the time, I had a sense of what was right, but I just plain didn't have the information to back up my instincts. This book is based on the research that supports your best instincts so that you can advocate for *your* child—or for your students—better than I did as a parent and as a teacher during my first stumbling efforts.

When Does Too Much Equal Worse than Nothing?

The other day while I was standing in line at my credit union, I noticed that behind the tellers, the bank had hung one of those huge billboards like the ones they have in Times Square with lines of digitized text scrolling the latest news. The words on that board march by in an unbroken stream, letter by letter—a format that makes it hard if not impossible to comprehend. But here's the worst part: entertainment news and other fluff all goose-stepped by on that bank billboard with the same authority as life-altering news events.

Even news programs now have a commentator reporting the latest news while at the same time, we are boggled by an unrelated scrolling text at the bottom of the screen. How does *anyone* comprehend this? How does anyone manage to listen to the news while reading a parade of disjointed letters and words that are unconnected to what the commentator is saying? It's like trying to focus on a strobe light.

I don't love standing in lines and I don't love traffic jams either, but those unsolicited moments of relative stillness used to force me to stay in one spot and to actually think for a while. I used to daydream while standing in the line of that bank and let my mind roam and think. Just think, that's all. Nothing else. Maybe hum a little tune or tap my fingers, but I was able to *think in peace*. When and how do we do that anymore? How do we unsmudge the truth and the relevant information from the trivia and the propaganda and evaluate it so it can inform, rather than confuse us about the choices we make in our lives?

So What's My Point and Why Don't I Hurry Up and Get to It?

Even as I'm writing this, a part of me is saying, "Hurry. Hurry. Get to the point. Tell them now what this has to do with the purpose of this book instead of *building* to the point. Make it shorter. Scroll that bottom line past them or they won't stay with you." I'm resisting that temptation and if you just stay with me, I think you'll see why.

So, let's put the scroll of information on "pause" for a minute and stop and just think. If *information* means we have access to facts that we can *trust to be true*, that are meaningfully communicated and that we can evaluate and use in our lives, then we live in the *illusion* of an information age. What we have in reality is like a mountain of files and papers unsorted in boxes—the kind that lawyers send to each other to create the illusion of fact sharing during court trials, knowing full well that the opposition will never be able to sift through it all.

And so it is with the avalanche of information that buries us daily. We will never have time to even open those boxes, much less sort through and distinguish the relevant from the trivial, much less decide if the so-called facts are credible or are just public relations or media spin or lies to promote some politician's or some corporation's own agenda. Would you agree that the too much, too fast assault of facts is actually the *antithesis* of information?

As a result of the staccato of clutter that so overwhelms us, we can't keep up with it all, and so in desperation, a lot of us have entrusted our responsibility to evaluate information and to look beneath the surface to a new growth industry—the Expert.

Experts

When was the last time you watched a news broadcast reporting some important event, or listened to a political speech, or to the report of the proceedings of a trial, or even to a sports event when the media did not produce an Expert to tell you what you'd just heard *and* interpret it for you? And after hearing the Expert, what stayed in your mind? Was it what you yourself noticed and thought and evaluated on your own, or did you almost without hesitation or reservation let the Expert do your thinking for you because your life is as hectic, as sadly cluttered, and rattles along as noisily as mine?

And now another question: How do we know that the Expert is not only technically qualified to think for us but also *ethical* enough to tell us the truth? When was the last time you stopped to ask yourself those questions? If your answer is "almost never" or even "I don't remember," then I suggest that in addition to the confetti of information we are buried under, we have created yet another layer of potential misinformation that broadens the ever widening gap between us and reality—or the relevant facts, if you will.

Transformations: Experts to Wizards

In the movie *The Wizard of Oz*, Dorothy, the Cowardly Lion, the Tin Man, and the Scarecrow travel down the Yellow Brick Road in search of the Wizard, whom they all believe has the power to solve their problems. He is the Expert transformed by what today we would call media spin into a Wizard. Someone in Oz started the rumor that he had wisdom and nearly superhuman powers, and the story was repeated with such frequency and such conviction that the Wizard of Oz was turned into an urban legend, in a process not unlike the way public relations firms and politicians and corporations spin or just out and out *create*—rather than report—the facts today.[2]

In the movie, Dorothy and her friends eventually find the Wizard of Oz, only to discover that he is nothing more than a little man behind a big curtain, pushing buttons, pulling switches, blowing smoke, and flashing mirrors. And so Dorothy discovers that the awe-inspiring, all-powerful authority figure, the Wizard, is just a human being like the rest of us and that his *real* power was the curtain. That is the first message of the movie.

Remember the story I shared about my first conference with my daughter's kindergarten teacher? I think for the first of many interactions with schools as a parent and as a teacher, my own insecurities elevated a person with a little bit of authority to the status of Wizard. When I walked into that kindergarten classroom, some kind of a transformation came over me. Or maybe it wasn't a transformation at all and what really happened was that I just reverted to who I really believed I was back then, all those years ago.

What I mean is that I was no longer an intelligent adult. I felt like a child again, nervous and intimidated by circumstances, by the surroundings, and, through no fault of her own, by the teacher behind the desk, which was for me, I guess—the equivalent of the big curtain. Looking back on it, I realize that for much of my adult life, I've felt like a not really competent teenager who was only pretending to be a grown-up. There's a word for this phenomenon in psychology. It's called *the imposter syndrome,* which refers to our tendency to feel that we are only acting at a new role in our life and that somehow, everyone else has some secret or knows something we don't. By surrendering to that syndrome, we actually help the Wizards hang their curtains.

As I related to you, I never did effectively make the points I needed to make with that teacher. I talked too fast and I tried too hard to impress her and to hide the fact that I was an imposter and was just playing the role that I believed still belonged to my own mom and dad—that of a good parent. And I succumbed to the same syndrome when I was a beginning teacher as well.

The World of School and the World of Life

I believe that part of the reason I felt so intimidated when talking to my daughter's teacher is because I'd been a student for so many years. I couldn't just pull a switch and transform into an adult in the same setting where I'd spent so many years as a child and then as an adolescent. And look at the setting. The rows of desks, the teacher's big desk, the bells and the clocks, even that school smell—I can't describe it, but I know that *you* know that smell as well as I do. They are all the trappings of order and of authority. We've all lived long stretches of our lives in schools like this and just stepping inside throws us back into *who* we were— when *we* were there—as students ourselves.

Obviously, society can't function without rules and some policing of those rules. The point I'm making and that I will refer back to later in this book is that there is a difference between LEGITIMATE authority and *figures* of authority who get their power from the EMPTY TRAPPINGS of authority. We need to understand that distinction. We need to remember also that in a democratic society, the citizens are participants in the rule making. We must have, if not the assurance, at least the possibility that our voices will be heard, acknowledged, and can evoke a change in governance. In other words, at the heart of a democracy is a fundamental need for and a belief in its responsiveness.

As a matter of fact, Chief Justice Jackson reminds us that it is our *responsibility* to question authority. He states, "It is *not* the function of the government to keep the citizen from falling into error; it is the function of the citizen to keep the *government* from falling into error." (Emphasis mine.)

Whether you realize it or not, it is now the federal government with all its power and its politics that is controlling the schools and the way our children view learning, how they feel about themselves, and consequently, who they will become as adults. As teachers and parents, it is our job to pull back the curtain and see just who is pulling switches, blowing smoke, and pushing our buttons.

How to Use This Book

You can read this book all the way through, or you can use it as a handbook by referring to the table of contents or the index for information about any given topic. What I hope is that as parents and teachers, you'll share this book with others and form discussion groups—or that you form these groups in your university classes—so that you can take back control of your own thinking. I want to provoke you and to challenge you, so that you become experts yourselves.

Why the Question-and-Answer Format?

I've used this format because many of the questions I answer in this book are those I had when I was a teacher and while my children were in school, and they are questions that parents and teachers are still asking today. This format also makes it easier for the reader to find information that he or she wants to revisit or to cite than does a long chapter of unbroken text.

More importantly though, it helps me feel more as if I'm having a true conversation with you instead of just scrolling words across an empty page. When I'm reading a book, part of what makes it a more satisfying experience for me than trying to read the scrolling text on the billboard in my bank or at the bottom of the television news broadcast is that I can slow my reading down.

And I ask questions aloud to myself or in my head—I question the author—as I read. And so here, I've tried to anticipate the questions you will raise, or in some cases, the questions I *hope* you will ask yourself as you read through this book. In part, these questions are a way of slowing us *both* down so we have time to think and so you can relate the ideas in this book to your own experiences. I want to clear the clutter, not add to it.

What Are the Endnotes?

At the end of some of the sentences in this book, you'll see a small number above the text. At any time, you can find that number at the section in the back of the book titled "Notes." Those numbers indicate the research sources for every fact I provide you so that you can confirm the information or use the sources when you yourself need to substantiate a point you are making with a teacher—or with a parent.

I hope you'll at least skim the endnotes. Sometimes I turn to the endnotes and just read them, almost as if they were part of the book, because often they provide interesting little tidbits of background information that the author doesn't want to clutter up the text with or that extend the point that the author is making.

The evidence-based facts in this book rely on the most current, reliable, scientific research available, including recent findings from brain research and government-financed studies on reading. As we have already discussed, human beings are not one-dimensional, so while I have based this book on the insights of respected, credible educators, I also rely on research from the fields of medicine and psychology. *But,* I don't want you to give over your power to those experts—or to me either, for that matter. My goal is give you the tools and the perspective to make the wisest choices for your children and students—*yourself.*

Pulling Down the Curtains

The first message in the *Wizard of Oz* is that the Wizard's power was actually just the curtain. But that first message is meaningless without the second message—Dorothy and her friends discover that the real power to change their lives was in them all the time. And that is what I hope you'll take away from this book. Not only do I want you to find the power to pull back the curtain, I want the Wizard to stand up when you enter the room.

Section II

BEHIND CURTAIN NUMBER 1: SCHOOL "REFORM"

Every breath you take, every move you make
. . . I'll be watching you.

—The Police, 1983[3]

SCANDAL!

Back in June of 2001, a huge scandal received nearly a week of national media coverage. The scandal did not involve the deceptions behind some international or domestic crisis. What happened was this: I know you've seen those on-the-street "spontaneous" interviews where moviegoers are questioned about their reactions to the movie they've just seen as they are exiting the theater. Well, through exhaustive investigative reporting, a journalist, Joe Horn, from *Newsweek* uncovered the truth: The director of creative advertising and another executive at Sony had fabricated the reviews of the movies *Vertical Limit, Hollow Man,* and *A Knight's Tale.* So instead of random interviews with *real* just-out-of-the-theater couples, in the commercials Sony aired, some of the "objective" reviewers actually worked for Sony.

Damage!

As a matter of fact, the damage done by the deception was so extensive that "two moviegoers lodged a class action lawsuit on behalf of millions of people who they claim were fooled into seeing *A Knight's Tale* by the fake reviews." The media assured us that

heads rolled at Sony as a result of the scandal and the two advertising executives responsible for planting the false reviews were
suspended for thirty days without pay.[4]

If you watched the news at all during June of 2001, you
couldn't possibly miss this story because it got extensive coverage
on the national evening news as well as on morning shows such
as the *Today Show*.

So What?

If you're asking, "So what? What's your point and what does this
have to do with school reform?" If you're thinking I'm making
some heavy-handed statement about the distorted priorities of
the media, you're only partly right. When I saw this story perme-
ating the news, my thought was, "Why don't these journalists direct their investigative energy into asking the *same questions* that
uncovered the Sony deception about a far greater scandal: the
deceptions, the planted reviews and research, and the vested
personal and financial interests that lurk behind the curtain of
school reform?"

Some journalists did indeed raise questions about school reform, but do you remember ever seeing any mainstream media
headlines about it? I don't. And the reason we didn't is because
the stories that *did* allude to any political or financial conflicts of
interest or to the possible negative repercussions of new education legislation mostly appeared in op-ed pieces on the education page—in stark contrast to the importance given the Sony
scandal.

Such tentative coverage hardly provided a visible—much less
viable—balance to the fanfare and media blitz that heralded
President Bush's education bill, No Child Left Behind. Why
didn't journalists apply the same investigative diligence to an education bill destined to impact every child, every parent, every
teacher, and every school in this country as they did to unearth-
ing and reporting deceptive movie reviews? Why?

ASKING THE RIGHT QUESTIONS

In this section, we're going to consider the questions that we
need to ask as we encounter stories and articles on schools because as we will see, we can't always rely on journalists to do it for

us. As I said in the introduction, I'm going to use a question-and-answer format here in the hope that it resembles as much of a true conversation as I can have with you, considering that you are an invisible reader. I hope it helps you be more actively involved in the process than if I had just scrolled a lot of information past you. "Your" questions are in italics.

I have read many articles exposing the miserable condition of public education. And you—like so many other critics of change—are opposing laudable efforts to reform this mess. Only today, I read a newspaper article, titled "Survey: Teachers See Selves as Scapegoats," on the need for school reform. The article cites a prominent educator, Chester Finn, who supports teacher accountability and high standards. It is clear from the high-quality research study the article cites that like you, most teachers are opposed to fixing up the mess they've made of the schools. Implied in Chester Finn's comments is the same question I am asking you: How dare *you or anyone else oppose vigorous efforts at improving schools?*[5]

Oh, I am in no way, shape, or form opposed to school reform. What I *am* opposed to, though, are ploys to destroy the public schools and the credibility of teachers in the *name* of school reform by Wizards hiding behind the curtain of research that cloaks their own political or even financial interests.

I'm going to spend some time addressing the article you mention—not because it's so important in and of itself—but because it's an example of how we can be deceived by the information that is scrolled past us in the media. I will now prove to you that we don't always know what we are reading and that we can't always trust journalists to ask the right questions.

You can skim the summary of the article that I provide here and see what questions pop up in your mind as you're reading. Then see if they are similar to the questions that I asked as I read it.

First, a Brief Summary of the Article

The article is written by Ben Fuller, who reports the findings of a research study that surveyed 1,345 teachers about the quality of schools and their feelings about school reform. It describes the groups that funded the study, one of which is the Thomas Fordham Foundation, as being bipartisan. So far so good, or so it seems.

The article reports that a large majority of teachers acknowledge that their school has some "bad" teachers and that it is very difficult to remove them because they are protected by the teachers unions. Furthermore, new teachers report that they are more willing to "embrace change" than veteran teachers.

Fuller includes reactions to the survey by members of the teachers union the National Education Association and Chester Finn, whom Fuller identifies as "president of the Fordham Foundation" (you remember—one of the "bipartisan" groups that conducted the research).

Here's How the Teachers' Side Is Presented in the Article
The research study the article cites indicates that teachers are becoming increasingly disenchanted with their profession because they are forced to spend less time teaching children because more time is required for test preparation; they also say that burgeoning federal regulations hobble their ability to make decisions in their classrooms. A large majority said that their school had some bad teachers who were protected by the union.

How Chester Finn's Side Is Presented in the Article
In response to the frustrations the teachers expressed in the survey, Chester Finn praises the Bush education plan with its focus on "accountability" and "high standards" and "alternatives" to public education as ways to redress the problems of failing schools and bad teachers. He then dismisses the concerns of the teachers who cooperated in the survey by saying they resist school reform and working to improve their teaching skills, and that they suffer from a "'woe-is-me' attitude about their lot in life."

The Subtle Messages Hiding Between the Lines
A cursory reading of the article leaves one with this impression: Even teachers acknowledge that schools have some bad teachers that the union protects, teachers whine about how hard their jobs are, and new teachers (Fuller might have chosen the word *inexperienced teachers*, but he didn't) are more willing to accept school reform, including charter schools and alternative teacher certification programs, than more entrenched teachers. Fuller de-

scribes teachers as "committed but frustrated." So both sides are represented, given a forum, and the article appears to be balanced.

Balanced? Whose Thumb Is on the Scale?

But this article is *unbalanced*, not so much for what it includes, but for what it omits. Now, here are the questions that arose in my mind as I read it. See if the answers change your perception of the survey's findings and how the article is subtly slanted in favor of Chester Finn because the journalist didn't ask the right questions—the same kinds of questions that helped uncover the Sony movie scandal.

The First Question/Observation That Arose as I Read the Article

The article mentions that Chester Finn is the president of the Thomas Fordham Foundation, one of the bipartisan groups that funded the survey. What other connections does he have?

Answer

Chester Finn was also the founding partner and senior scholar of Edison Project from 1992 through 1994, a for-profit corporation designed to replace free, public education with the help of the federal government. Therefore, Chester Finn serves to profit by eliminating public education so "alternative" schools such as Edison can move in and take over public education as well as teacher accreditation. This is a fact, plain and simple. Is it any wonder, then, that Finn praises the Bush education plan, since they share so many common goals of school reform? Doesn't Finn's review of the research findings remind you of the conflict of interest we saw in the fabricated reviews in the Sony commercials?

Chester Finn: Reformist or Exterminator?

Finn is frequently cited in educational publications and news articles, and almost without exception, he attacks public education and teachers. And yet, I have never seen an article in a mainstream publication even mention, much less suggest, that his attacks on education might stem from his own interests in Edison. Given that his corporation stands to profit if public schools are eliminated, shouldn't we wonder if Finn's attacks on education may not be an effort to *improve* public schools but rather one to *eliminate* them? Didn't this journalist wonder about this, too?

Oh, by the way, if you are questioning *my* facts, well, good for you! Go to Google and type in "Chester Finn" and "Edison Project" and see for yourself. But wait! There's more.

The Second Question/Observation That Arose as I Read the Article

Maybe Finn's corporate interests do indeed diminish the credibility of his frequent attacks on teachers and schools. However, it could be that with the Edison schools, he has discovered the magic bullet for educating children. So maybe he is an enlightened educator, and for-profit schools such as those run by Edison Schools are really *the answer* to the education crisis.

Answer

Edison schools have failed repeatedly. Here's just one example: Two of the three Edison-run schools in West Baltimore showed heartbreaking drops in children's academic performance. *Not one third grader passed the test in math, reading, social studies, or science, and fifth graders declined in every subject!* This is in spite of the huge salary of nine hundred thousand dollars and millions of dollars in stock options for Edison Schools' director. In Baltimore alone, two out of three Edison schools failed our children. Remember, this is but one example of Edison's failure.[6]

And yet Finn's attacks are directed at teachers and public schools instead of at his own corporate enterprise. Does it strike you, then, that he applies his altruistic concerns for accountability and high standards somewhat prejudicially? Why isn't this question raised in the article?

The Third Question/Observation That Arose as I Read the Article

So Edison schools are failures, but other corporations might bring the efficiency of their business practices into education and my child would benefit, right?

Answer, and a Question for You: Who Do You Trust to Care for Your Child?

Look at the corporate business models we've seen in this country and the ethical and moral decisions business leaders have made.

If you were the president of a large corporation that was running the schools, what would your priorities be? How would you want to see children develop and learn? Would you want to encourage critical thinkers who would evaluate and ask questions and who might even question the ethics of *your* business practices? Or would you incorporate methods that would mold children into passive, obedient workers who would not make waves and challenge your methods?

One more point to consider. In case you're hesitating over your answers to the questions I pose here, ask yourself this: I don't know what your job is, but how receptive is your boss or administrator to *your* ideas and challenges to his ethics or business practices? Does the corporation you work for operate with *your* best interests in mind? Now—imagine the bottom-line mentality of business moguls and Wall Street entrepreneurs helping to shape your child's future. Do you trust the Enrons of the world enough to hand your children over to them? I don't.

The Fourth Question/Observation That Arose as I Read the Article

One of the funders of the survey in the article was the Fordham Foundation. So the study was based on legitimate research and we can trust the findings, right?

Answer

Wrong. First, the president of the Fordham Foundation is Chester Finn, who would like to see the end of public education, remember? So, at the outset, shouldn't we question how bipartisan the foundation's involvement is, based on that fact alone? Second, the article doesn't mention that the Fordham Foundation is an organization with a very focused ideological and even financial agenda. Therefore, even if you agree with its right-wing political agenda, by definition, it is not bipartisan. Incidentally, another officer of the Fordham Foundation is Diane Ravitch, another very vocal, highly visible, "bipartisan" school "reformer." Tip: When *anyone* shouts, "Bipartisan!" watch out.

The Fifth Question/Observation That Arose as I Read the Article

How do we know that the research data in the study, or in any other research study, is accurate and honestly reported?

Answer

We don't.

One More Observation: Exploitation in the Name of Reform

I can't think of a way to pose this as a question, but it's an observation I made as I read the article, and it's worth noting. As
we've observed, the teachers cooperated in this study that was
funded in part by the Fordham Foundation, of which Chester
Finn (Edison mogul) is president. What was the teachers' reward
for being nice enough to answer the questions in the survey in
the good-faith belief that they were helping education?

The answer? In no way does Chester Finn acknowledge that
any of their concerns are legitimate. He demeans them as a group
and trivializes their frustrations. Finn reduces these committed
teachers to a bunch of whiners with a "'woe-is-me' attitude about
their lot in life."

Thus, in addition to being of questionable objectivity, the survey carries with it more than a whiff of exploitation, not only
of the research process itself but of the teachers who were generous enough to participate. In good faith, those teachers handed
Chester Finn yet another club to batter them with. I'm actually
embarrassed for him.

So once again, we need to ask, Isn't Chester Finn's "review" of
the research and teachers and schools at least as tainted (by his
own self-interests) as the false movie reviews in the Sony scandal? Isn't this issue more important, too?

*So . . . I think what you're saying is that asking Chester Finn
for advice on improving schools is like asking a fox to conduct
self-help seminars for chickens. Right?*

I like that metaphor. I like the Wizard metaphor too, though.

The Bottom Line: Look Behind the Curtain for the *Real* Story

As I mentioned earlier, this article in and of itself is not so important. Chances are, relatively few people will ever read it, and
Chester Finn is *only one* of the foxes conducting better-living
seminars for chickens.

The point is, though, that the *real* story never got reported,
and the *important* questions never got asked, and this happens in

hundreds of news reports over hundreds of days, and it colors the thinking of millions of Americans. This phenomenon is played out with such alarming regularity that propaganda and out-and-out lies eventually transmute into fact. And so it is that urban legends are created and Wizards (and foxes) are free to flourish.

Protect Your Child: Question Everything and Everyone

I won't insult you by asking you if you believe that issues affecting our children's future are more important than whether people are duped into seeing a bad movie based on fabricated reviews and misleading statements. Of course you do. But, I will ask you why that Sony exposé was treated to so prominent a position in the media while so little scrutiny is afforded to who's pushing our buttons on so-called school reform. I'm willing to bet that the majority of Americans think that school reform is just what it claims to be: change for the betterment of the public schools, teachers, and kids.

Since I should question everyone and everything, how do I know I can trust you?

You don't. You don't know me well enough yet for me to answer this right now. Ask me again later in the book.

The Important Questions We Need to Ask

Whether you are a parent or a teacher, or even a journalist, I hope you ask the following questions of any media story that you encounter—or that encounters *you*. Furthermore, I hope you model thinking through issues and asking questions such as these with your children because—as we will see later—school reform is threatening to make sure they don't do much thinking, questioning, evaluating, or challenging in their classrooms anymore.

Here are the questions you need to ask so you can protect your child and your rights as parents and teachers:

- How do you know that?
- What evidence do you have to support that claim?
- What is the source of that evidence?

- How do you know that the evidence you are reporting (or reading here) is true?
- What underlying motives may color the veracity of the information provided by your source?
- Who stands to profit financially from this claim?

BEWARE OF BUZZWORDS!

You've probably also noticed by now that official-sounding buzzwords such as *reform, accountability, standards, research, institute* and *foundation, scientifically proven methods,* and *report of the National Reading Panel (NRP)* help hold up the curtain for the Wizard. In fact, I hope that any time you encounter any of these words, you *mentally put quotation marks around them.*

Beware also of news articles touting the success of some "scientifically proven" program, because advertisements distributed by corporations are often disguised as legitimate news stories. For example, here's a headline about Voyager Learning, one of the government's approved programs:

FOR IMMEDIATE RELEASE
November 13, 2002
VOYAGER UNIVERSAL LITERACY SYSTEM BEING UTILIZED IN NINE HOUSTON SCHOOLS
New Report Shows System Delivered Unprecedented Reading Gains[7]

On the surface, this headline and the article that follows it look like a legitimate news bulletin. The "news" story that follows this headline cites "independent research" showing that Voyager provided enormous gains for children. But if we ask the questions we've just listed here, here's what we find: The "independent" research the article touts was orchestrated by Joseph Torgesen, who just happens to be part of the Voyager design team. It also doesn't mention that this is a press release by the company itself and that Jerri Nowakowski, who is listed as the contact person, like Torgesen, is part of the Voyager design team.[8]

The blurring of news and infomercials and propaganda is exacerbated by the fact that sometimes legitimate journalists pick up such stories, and because they may lack the background knowledge to make informed judgments, repeat the corporate claims in their own columns. Thus, they become accomplices to perpetuating and feeding the public relations machines that create urban legends.

Two major reading programs that are mining the school market and use the ploy of "research" through strategically planted "news" stories are McGraw-Hill's Open Court and *Language!* distributed by Sopris West/McGraw-Hill/Glencoe. We'll look more closely at the entrepreneurial "scientific" researchers that have reviewed these programs and their links to government-approved reading methods later in this book.

As we will see now, the most deceptive buzzword of all is the *sweeping reform* (buzzword) of No Child Left Behind (lie). We'll now look at the Bush education plan that Chester Finn praises and pull down that curtain.

BEHIND THE CURTAIN OF NO CHILD LEFT BEHIND

Every breath you take, every move you make . . . every step you take—I'll be watching you.

The Police, 1983

I'm writing these words in June of 2003 even though you're reading them much later than that because it takes months from the time a book is completed until it goes into print. Therefore, it's usually tricky to comment on some current political situation because it may radically change by the time a book gets into the hands of readers.

No Relief in Sight

Sad to say, though, I have every confidence (and not in a good way) that what I'm writing about No Child Left Behind (NCLB) at this very moment will be relevant even if you're reading this five or even ten years after it was written. I doubt that NCLB will have disappeared by the time you read this, but even if it were abolished this very day, our children and our schools would still be reeling from the harmful effects of this legislation for years into the future.

You need to know this too. When I say that NCLB will eviscerate the public schools and harm many of our children, particularly minorities and the children of the poor, I'm not exaggerating. And I'm not wrong, either.

Why should I spend my time trying to understand No Child Left Behind?

The effects of NCLB extend to every level of education. In fact, Reid Lyon, President Bush's education advisor, stated publicly, "If I were in charge of making the laws, I'd blow up the colleges of education."[9] We're in for a lot of major changes at many levels. They aren't abstract and distant. They are here and they are now and they affect our children and their teachers.

Just the Facts on No Child Left Behind

No Child Left Behind is a law. It was by signed by President Bush in January 2002.[10] It is a sweeping piece of federal legislation that controls instructional methods, materials, and what teachers can do and say in their classrooms. Therefore, it profoundly affects your child or, if you're a teacher, the children in your care.

Hiding in Plain Sight

The NCLB document itself includes hundreds of pages of legal jargon and amendments, and it is impossible to read. It is like trying to read one of those deliberately obtuse legal documents or one of those helpful public service booklets the Internal Revenue Service distributes to help us understand the tax laws.

Some parts of NCLB contradict other sections. I humbly suggest that its inaccessibility may be deliberate. In other words, no one involved is accountable for anything because this law says *whatever* the Wizards want it to say, *whenever* they want to say it. Here, though, are the main components of the law that have been forced upon schools; you can just skim this list if you want, but here it is for you to reference:

Main Components of No Child Left Behind

- Control of schools and teachers is maintained by legislated standards, mandates, and increased "teacher accountability" as determined by scores on standardized tests.

- Districts whose scores don't meet the standard are designated as "failing" or "low-performing" schools. If they don't raise their test scores, they are either closed or the government moves in and takes them over. Parents then send their children elsewhere, including private and charter schools.
- If you are just skimming this list, *pay attention to this!* Private schools, including for-profit schools run by corporations, are not held to the same standards or the same accountability as the public schools. In other words, schools such as Edison schools (you remember, Chester Finn's brainchild) can fail—and continue to fail our children—without a peep from the same federal government that is strangling public education in the name of high standards and leaving no child behind. Are you starting to see a pattern here?
- Public schools that are declared to be failures can opt not to comply with the mandates of NCLB, but if they don't comply, the federal government will withhold money, thus ensuring that they can't continue unless they obey the mandates. Private schools can do pretty much anything they want.
- The instructional methods and materials imposed on low-performing or failing schools *are not the same methods* that are used by high-performing (usually more affluent) schools. Thus, children in low-performing schools receive a more back-to-basics, dumbed-down curriculum instead of the methods that are used in high-performing schools and that may have made them successful in the first place.
- Parents of children who don't make the grade can have their children tutored with some government support, but only if they allow their children to be trained by those agencies or programs the federal government approves of.
- Low-performing schools can apply for federal monies through Reading First grants. In order to get the grant, though, the schools need to use government-approved

materials and teachers must be trained by government-approved professional providers.

- NCLB contains a local control clause that prohibits government interference in the business of school. And so NCLB breaks its own law! It states:

Nothing in this section shall be construed to:
1. authorize an officer or employee of the federal government to mandate, direct, *review*, or control a state local educational agency or schools' instructional content, curriculum, and related *activities*;
2. limit the application of the General Education Provisions Act to require the distribution of scientifically or medically false or inaccurate material or to prohibit the distribution of scientifically or medically true or accurate materials. (Emphasis mine.)

You keep repeating the idea of the federal government taking over the schools as if that is a bad thing. Why are you so threatened by it?

I just finished reading a book by Seymour Sarason, who is in his eighties at this writing and who has witnessed years of educational folly and failed school reforms.[11] He makes a point that I had never considered in quite the way he frames it. What he notes is that the colonists broke off from England because they recognized the dangers of being governed by a monarchy thousands of miles away that had no knowledge of, much less respect for, how they lived their personal and working lives.

True Patriots

The colonists believed "if those who govern you do not and cannot know you, then the needs and the liberties of the governed are at best endangered and at worst extinguished."[12] Our forefathers were true patriots. They valued—indeed, they fought for—the rights of the individual against an arrogant and intrusive government that had its own agenda. They would have fought against No Child Left Behind.

The Federal Government Is Usurping Your Rights as Parents

It was literally inconceivable to the framers of the Constitution that the national government should have anything to do with parental rights—those of overseeing the education and the values of our children. Such intrusion would at best be based on ignorance. At worst it would pose a threat to freedom.[13]

In totalitarian countries ruled by dictators, the government controls the schools. It is obvious why. Control the schools, mandate the curriculum, control the teachers, and you have brainwashed the next generation. That's how dictators operate. It is exactly what the colonists fought *against*, isn't it?

Now please turn back to that bulleted list of the tenets of NCLB. Look at that last bulleted statement, the one on local control. That is a direct quote from the law. You can see that the law itself *prohibits the federal government from even reviewing, much less recommending, much less mandating, curriculum*. In other words, it would appear that those Wizards who framed the NCLB legislation agreed with our founding fathers and that the federal government has no business usurping parental rights by controlling the public schools, right?

And now I want to plant the seeds of a big question for you to keep in mind from this moment on. If you're discussing this book as part of a book group, consider raising this question periodically in response to policies and political actions that don't make sense:

> Is it possible that the federal government—like Chester Finn—is not interested in reforming public education but wants to eliminate it in the name of reform so private corporations can profit from your tax dollars and control the lives of our children?
>
> Don't decide on an answer now. Just keep the question in mind.

Since NCLB makes it illegal for representatives or employees of the federal government to interfere in how we choose to educate our children, I don't see how you can cry, "Federal interference!" Aren't you way off base here?

I need to inject a personal note here before I get down to business and answer that question. I emailed my friends Lois Bridges and Ardie Cole to say that as I write this book, there are times I have to confront hypocrisies that are so outrageous they make me choke out loud. When that happens, my cat, who sits next to me as I pound away on my laptop, flies off the sofa and cowers in a corner. When I wrote that bulleted quote about local control, copied directly from NCLB, my cat actually hissed at me, maybe because he thought I hissed at him first. Take a look at the rest of those bulleted statements. Does that sound like a bill respecting individual rights and honoring local control to you? Now, I'll answer your question, but you won't like the answer.

And Now, My Answer to Your Question

Remember I told you at the beginning of this section that there are convenient contradictions in NCLB as well as in the way it's presented to the country? Here is how it works: Spokespersons for the U.S. Department of Education claim that the federal government is *not* imposing anything on the schools at all. Heaven forbid. Schools are free to make their own decisions. They don't need to use the materials and the methods that the government claims are scientifically proven. It's just that if schools reject the mandates, well . . . they don't get federal funding.

Your Tax Dollars at Work

I'm including a quote here by the secretary of education of the United States of America about what schools need to do to get federal money to help them meet the needs of your child. If you want to just skim this, fine—I've italicized the most important words. I'm including it here so you can see that I am not exaggerating how much NCLB will affect your child, *and* that schools *must* go along with it if they want to survive:

> Through Reading First, schools **will implement instructional programs and materials** based on this research. Program materials and activities **must** meet the criteria for scientifically based reading research outlined in the legislation and discussed in the program guidance. In their applications for Reading First funds, State educational agencies **must** outline the specific criteria they will use to evaluate the suitability of programs and materials.

> *These applications **will be reviewed** by an expert panel that **will make recommendations** for funding or for disapproval in accordance with the law.*[14] (Emphasis mine.)

Now, let's flip back to that bulleted list and look at the law of local control again. There is no ambiguity in the wording. Look at the statement by our secretary of education. Does this sound to you as if the federal government is adhering to the law of local control that out and out prohibits any employee from reviewing, much less recommending, "a . . . school's instructional content, curriculum and related activities"?

Coercing "Choice"

In truth, NCLB amounts to saying to schools in desperate need of funds, "Do what we tell you or we'll cut off your arms and legs, gag you, cover you with honey, and stake you to an anthill in the blazing sun without food and water until you die. But please, please . . . there's no pressure here. After all, you have local control. How could *anyone* possibly get the idea that our federal government is controlling the education of your children in direct opposition to what our forefathers fought for? My goodness. How *do* these rumors get started!"

But I've heard that parents have more choices in their children's education than ever before with No Child Left Behind. Isn't it true that the federal government will pay for sending children to private schools and wants to offer Opportunity Scholarships? Isn't that a good thing?

That's a good question. Let's take a realistic look at school vouchers, Opportunity Scholarships, and whose children are left behind by these "reforms." On July 29, 2003, our secretary of education, Rod Paige, who is paid to represent *all* children, wrote a remarkable letter to the *Wall Street Journal*. In it, he blasted schools in Washington, D.C., for their latest NAEP scores because, like those across much of the country, they've dropped since President Bush's NCLB was signed into law. Paige describes the schools as "debilitated" and part of a "debilitating system." Furthermore, Paige states:

> It's impossible to track the gap between the rich and poor, between the white and African American kids because, we

can't track this gap over time since by 8th grade there aren't enough white students in the D.C. public schools to constitute a statistically significant subgroup. *That's likely because parents with the means to get their kids out of D.C. public schools* choose *to do so.* Parents who want to give their children a better education but can't afford to pay for it are left without choices.[15] (Emphasis mine.)

So what is the solution? Who among us would suggest *this?*

"Hmmm, rich parents can afford to get their kids out of crumbling schools. Parents who can't afford private schools want choices, too. So, I know! We'll give Opportunity Scholarships to two thousand poor children and brag about how compassionate we are. This one-year scholarship is less than two thousand dollars for each child and won't cover the total tuition for even one year, but the poor parents of these children will be so grateful that they will pick up the rest of the tab. This ingenious, 'compassionate' move then 'would force the entrenched local education establishment to reform and improve.'" Do you sense as I do a cavalier, "let them eat cake" choplogic to this strategy?

The first flaw that is obvious to many of us who struggle to make ends meet is that Paige's proposed legislation *leaves more than sixty-five thousand children behind in those schools that he himself says are debilitated!*[16]

Second, how can parents living in poverty possibly pick up the rest of the tab when the definition of *poverty* is "lack of money"?

Third, Paige's grand plan proposes that this legislation will somehow manage to bludgeon already "debilitated schools" into getting undebilitated. Thus, he not only blames the victim but punishes the victim for good measure. Good grief! How can school vouchers do anything but increase the gap between the rich and the poor and extend the inequities in the education system that already exist?

Isn't it perhaps telling that Paige's compassionate gesture designed to put money in the coffers of private, for-profit schools appears in the *Wall Street Journal,* a publication that is probably not the newspaper of choice for the poor people to whom he wants to extend "choice"?

Notice too, Paige's use of the term *debilitating system* in referring to the public schools. Does that suggest to you that, like Chester Finn's suggested "reforms," the goal here is not to help

public education, but to set up an alternative system of privatized, unregulated schools, let the poor be damned or eat cake, or
get undebilitated on their own—or whatever?

One more really important point about school reform. The
money is not there to pay for all of the proposals and the Reading
First grants and the increased testing that sit at the black heart of
NCLB. In fact, former undersecretary of education Neuman,
who resigned her position in January 2003, stated that one of her
reasons for resigning was that there was not enough money to
pay for all the reforms proposed by President Bush's NCLB legislation.

In fact, the monetary outlook for NCLB is so grim that the
National Education Association, the nation's largest teachers
union, threatened to sue the federal government because teachers and districts are acting in good faith, devoting enormous
amounts of work and time to comply to legislation that doesn't
have the money to back up its big promises.[17]

One stark example of the impracticality of NCLB, to say
nothing of its heartlessness, is how NCLB is hurting children in
Alaska. There, schools in isolated villages have been declared as
"failing." The government's required redistribution of children
to "better" schools entails not just money that isn't there but
boarding students away from home and family. Most Alaskan
communities are accessible only by air. It's not just difficult. It's
impossible to commute and imposes a heartless burden on students who would be required to live away from home for the
years needed to complete school.[18]

Such casual disregard for children puts me in mind of a quote
by a true scientist, Albert Einstein, who never lost sight of the
ethical, moral, and human imperatives that must not be sacrificed in the name of science to promote selfish political agendas:

"WHAT NEED IS THERE FOR A CRITERION OF RESPONSIBILITY?
I believe that the horrifying deterioration in the ethical conduct of people today stems primarily from the mechanized de-
humanization of our lives—a disastrous byproduct of the
development of the scientific and technical mentality. . . .
Man grows cold faster than the planet he inhabits."

Albert Einstein, letter to Dr. Otto Juliusburger,
April 11, 1946

The Bottom Line on No Child Left Behind

Schools and teachers are threatened with deprivation so extensive that it is in truth coercion. Even if NCLB were an equitable reform—and it is not—it couldn't work anyway. The money to implement it is not there. Your child's future is not in your hands. It is under the control of the federal government and major corporations. Period.

Questions for Discussion: Assuming that the government does not have the money to back its legislation, as Neuman and NEA assert, what does this mean for the schools and for the teachers who worked to complete Reading First grant proposals and spent their time struggling to comply with the mandates? What is the practical effect of school vouchers and Opportunity Scholarships on poor and middle-class children as opposed to the children of the wealthy? What does this mean for public education? If public education fails due to bad legislation, false promises, and a lack of funding, who wins? Who loses?

But I like the idea of leaving no child behind. Maybe that is really what the federal government wants to do. Maybe it is just a difference in interpretation. You are running around yelling, "The sky is falling! Watch out! Conspiracy!" On the other hand, maybe the feds are really trying to find a way to help all children, a noble goal that even the colonists would have applauded.

Oh, I love the ideal of leaving no child behind, too. But the *ideal* and the *law* of the No Child Left Behind act are in opposition. In other words, they are fundamentally incompatible. Here's why. The whole NCLB act is riveted in place by extensive, exhaustive testing of our kids—all done in the name of another big buzzword that holds up another heavy curtain—*accountability*.

Section III

BEHIND THE CURTAIN OF ACCOUNTABILITY: ALL ABOUT TESTING

Now, it is the view of the Ministry that a theoretical knowledge will be more than sufficient to get you through your examination, which, after all, is what school is all about.

—Professor Umbridge in *Harry Potter and the Order of the Phoenix*[19]

Why is the ideal of leaving no child behind incompatible with the law of No Child Left Behind? Why in the world would you be opposed to accountability?

Do you remember the movie *The Music Man* and the famous song sung by Robert Preston: "Ya got trouble. . . right here in River City with a capital *T* and that rhymes with *P* and that stands for *pool*"?[20] In that movie, the music man creates a false crisis so he can then sell the cure. The crisis is that a pool table has come to town and the cure is a boys band that Robert Preston sells but doesn't have the skill or the means to actually produce. His pattern has been to create the crisis, sell the cure, and then leave town.

With NCLB, it works like this: We do a lot of testing. This is a good thing right off the bat because testing profits the test preparation companies. We make the stakes high; kids' futures depend on it. We spin this as *high standards* and *accountability*. However,

29

since the tests are *standardized*, we 100 percent guarantee that no matter what, half the kids will be declared below average. In "model" states, like Florida, we've even managed to make more than half the kids below average. So now we can sing, "Trouble, trouble, trouble. What to do, what to do . . ."

Now, we provide the cure. We have this crisis that we've created. So far so good. But how can we make sure teachers and teacher preparation programs don't use their own methods and materials instead of ours?

OK. We'll declare that only schools that use "scientifically proven" programs can receive grants. And we shall call those grants what? . . . What's a good name that has an academic *and* a compassionate cachet? Oh, yes. *Reading First*. But, how do we prove that the programs we want to sell are scientifically proven? Eureka! We'll create panels of "scientific experts." But how to do it, how to do it . . . ? Some of the best scientists and researchers won't support this. OK. We'll just make sure that the Reading First expert panel and the National Reading Panel are with us on this. And a good way to make sure of that is to appoint a lot of "scientists" with their own programs to sell or who can work as "consultants" and sell their professional development services to districts that want our approval. And if anyone notices this, well, we'll just deny it and the public will listen to what we plant in the media.

And now that we have this major crisis, we can also start a new growth industry of *supplemental programs* sold by private corporations that are very nice to us. No matter that regardless of how many kids we send to summer school or to Sylvan Learning or who work on Voyager Learning programs, 50 percent of the kids and schools will still be below average. That just keeps the crisis going because we'll just make a lot of noise and make sure the accountability all flows downhill. We'll blame the stupid teachers and the failing public schools. We'll just keep wringing our hands, declaring our compassion, oiling our public relations machine, and by the time it all collapses, we'll be there with for-profit schools to pick up the pieces. And what's so great is that we don't just win at the end, we win all the way along the line. It's win, win, win for the people who matter.

That's a very strong statement presented with a lot of passion. I can't agree with your cynical view of accountability and of

our scientific researchers and leaders. I also don't understand how we will always have at least 50 percent of our kids and schools below average, as you claim. Can you back up these accusations?

The plan I've outlined is indeed very passionately stated, but it's not overstated. Let's look at the facts and then you can decide. Since a key pin in the plan I've outlined is accountability, we need to look at standardized testing. I know you've heard the term *standardized testing*. It's become so much a part of our system of education that we don't even necessarily stop to think of what it means anymore. So here is a lesson.

TESTING 101

First, we need to understand that there are many different kinds of testing models and that they serve different purposes.

Criterion-Referenced Tests: Personal Growth or Personal Best Versus Child Against Child

Some tests look at children's performance over time on a particular skill. A child's performance is measured against how she's done before. For example, we may keep track of how many laps a child can swim. In a classroom setting, a teacher might design a test to see if students understand a concept. The teacher returns the tests to the students so they know their scores and what areas they need to work on and the teacher knows how she needs to redirect her instruction. These kinds of tests are called *criterion-referenced* tests.[21] Sometimes, but not always, criterion-referenced tests are used with another type of performance-based assessment called a *student portfolio*.

Student Portfolios: Authentic Assessment

I've heard a lot about portfolio assessment. What is it and how does it compare to criterion-referenced tests?

A student portfolio is a systematic, selective overview of a student's work that is gathered by the student and the teacher over a period of time. Portfolios represent a comprehensive, multifaceted picture of actual student work so that teachers and students can plan *together* to set goals and establish academic priorities. They stand in contrast to test scores that provide a narrow, artificial, and possibly inaccurate peek at one facet of *test performance* that may or may not truly reflect *growth* or even *learning*. Often, the student and the teacher present the portfolio to the parents in a conference. Thus, with portfolios, the student is part of the process, so that assessment is done *with* rather than *on* the student.

These portfolios can include some teacher-made tests, or even standardized test scores, but they often include personal examples of a child's progress, such as samples of his writing over a period of time or a list of the books he's read and his responses to them. They may also contain running records that document not just a child's reading level but the *kinds* of errors, or miscues, he makes as he reads so the teacher and the child can *focus on specific, very personalized instructional needs*. Portfolio assessments offer a complete, comprehensive picture of a student's application of skills rather than an artificial slice of performance on a single measure of ability at a single moment in time. Because they are a collection of actual student work rather than just a test score— which may or may not reflect the actual learning and abilities of a student—portfolios are sometimes referred to as a type of *authentic assessment.*

authentic progress.

Ideally, student portfolios inform teachers, students, and parents of authentic student progress, how a student thinks, makes decisions, and organizes and approaches real-life tasks. Portfolios are personal and celebratory rather than impersonal, removed from authentic skills application, and possibly punitive—as test scores can be.

I like to view portfolios as the type of school work that we hang on the refrigerator and save to look at years later. My mother has a cedar chest full of my poems, stories, projects, and artwork that date clear back to my days in kindergarten more than fifty years ago! I don't think she saved a single test score. That cedar chest is my student portfolio. It means a lot to my mom—and to me, too.

I think I'm beginning to understand why you value student portfolios. They are very personal and probably do reflect my child's accomplishments and abilities better than just test scores. But I think you slid over the potential problems with criterion-referenced tests. During my years as a student, I've

been a victim of a lot of bad criterion-referenced tests made up by bad teachers. I still have nightmares about it. So what's your point?

Of course, we've all experienced some problems with criterion-referenced tests. Maybe the questions designed by your teacher were too hard or too easy or maybe the questions didn't really address the underlying concept. One teacher's grading scale or priorities could very well be different from another teacher's. We all remember teachers who had a reputation for being hard or easy. But at least there was a connection between *you* ⟶ and the *teacher* ⟶ and the *test*. And if you thought a question was unfair, you could (unless the teacher was a real hardnose) raise your hand and respectfully question your score. I've done that over the years and my students sometimes catch errors on the tests *I* make up. I listen. And then if I've made a mistake or if I've written a confusing question, I fix it.

As we're about to see, the same problems that we may have experienced with bad teacher-made tests plague standardized tests as well—including bad, ambivalent questions and questions that test trivia. Furthermore, there are sometimes serious errors in the scoring. But unlike the bad teacher-made tests we may have experienced, with standardized tests, there is no personal connection or contact between the test maker and the hapless test takers.

I'm sure you won't ignore those "serious" problems with standardized tests, but first I need to understand how teacher-made, criterion-referenced tests differ from the standardized tests that we hear so much about.

Standardized tests retain the same flaws as criterion-referenced tests, but they have way more clout and are far more dangerous to our children than any bad teacher-made test. I think it's fair to say that they are the testing equivalent of the remote, detached, and impersonal type of central governance that the colonists fought against and that we discussed in Section 2 of this book. The tests are *standardized* because one of the goals is to make sure that large numbers of children are tested using the same questions and are scored by the same criteria. The goal, **ideally,** is to ensure that the same scale is used to assess all the children in a group. However, the cliché "garbage in, garbage out" applies with a vengeance.

Well, then, standardized tests seem like a reasonable solution to the quirks and whims of teacher-made or criterion-referenced tests. So why is your cat cowering in the corner?

Yes, we've all had good tests and bad tests that teachers prepared for us. We've all also experienced those big paper-and-pencil tests such as the SATs and those little fill-in-the-boxes-with-a-number-two-pencil-multiple-choice-type tests that we had to take occasionally in school. You recall that they were snatched from our hands and from our teachers' hands, sent away to be scored, never to be seen again, although some invisible Wizard recorded our performance on them. Those were standardized tests.

What's happened is that the importance and the sheer volume of standardized tests have ballooned until they have buried schools, crippled teachers, and hurt our children. In other words, the stakes have been upped, and now, the tail is wagging the dog. Or as nationally known child advocate Alfie Kohn notes, "Children are burnt at the high stakes."[22]

Here are the problems with the whole testing scene.

What's at Stake?

The hallmark of standardized tests is the fact that they compare children with one another, and now that the stakes are upped, they compare teachers and schools too, so we have a system of education based on "winners" and "losers." *Thus, the very essence of the standardized testing system requires that many children will be left behind!*

What are some of the most common standardized tests?

The most common are the Iowa and the Stanford, Metropolitan, and California Achievement Tests—otherwise known as the SAT, the MAT, and the CAT, respectively.[23]

No Mercy

There are so many dangers inherent in the threat of standardized tests that it's hard to know where to start. Remember that these standardized tests are now mandated by the federal government if schools are to get monies. "Low-performing" schools, usually those in poor neighborhoods, are closed or are taken over by the federal government based on their scores. Private schools and those for-profit schools run by big business corporations are exempt from the same standards that apply to the public schools. Those tests are high-stakes because they are used to control curriculum, punish teachers, and label and sort our children. In fact, vital, life-altering decisions such as whether or not they will graduate and get their diplomas often hinge on a single test score.

Unreliable Results

Suppose a child is having a bad day, or is not feeling well, or simply doesn't perform well under pressure. Have you ever choked during a timed test, or somehow been unable to retrieve the information that you needed and ended up with a score that did not accurately reflect your true grasp of the subject matter? If that happens to a child during one of those testing situations that can determine his fate, then there is no chance for redemption. There is no court of appeal because the testing culture is cold, faceless, and ruthless. It is not a personal and compassionate approach to any child's unique needs.

Also, haven't you played the "test game" and spent more time trying to figure out what the Wizard who constructed that standardized test question was *thinking* when he constructed it instead of "What's *really* the *best* answer here?" I remember doing that. And I also remember playing a kind of psychological game of chess with the mysterious Wizard who wrote the questions on the SATs when I took them. I'll bet you've done that too.

Some children are naïve enough to believe that school and tests make sense and may not be able to play that game as well as some of us did. Young children below grade four are particularly vulnerable to the vagaries of formulaic responses. This is because young children develop quickly and along differing time scales, and so determining their futures and labeling them based on their arbitrary performance on an arbitrary test given at one fixed point in time is a travesty of our trust in the education system.

The term that refers to the *consistency* of a child's test performance—or to put it another way, the likelihood that the child or a similar group of test takers would perform about as well if the test were taken at a different time—is *reliability*. The examples I gave here as possible factors that can interfere with students' ability to perform in a manner that will accurately and consistently represent their true ability are roadblocks to reliability—the testing law that states that the results must be incorruptible and virtually invariable. Therefore, because so much depends on the results, if a student has a bad day or is actually very intelligent but is just a plain bad test taker, she doesn't get another shot at it, and so the high stakes may actually escalate the chances of unreliability.

Are Standardized Tests Valid?

Test questions are frequently multiple choice so that there's no opportunity for children to construct their own answers, much less explain their thinking. And after all, isn't it supposed to be *thinking* that we value instead of a confetti of useless facts?

Do you remember Dustin Hoffman's character Raymond in the movie *Rain Man*? He had a lot of dates and numbers in his head, but he was unable to put them to any practical use. Raymond's "knowledge" was nothing more than a pile of useless facts—a kind of parlor trick. He could compute complex mathematical problems in his head and he could count the number of spilled toothpicks that hit the floor, but it was most definitely his brother who was the brains of the outfit because he was the thinker who could put the skills to use.

When a test doesn't actually measure what it claims to, we say that it's lacking in *validity*. For example, if we gave Raymond a test that claimed to measure his ability to apply mathematical concepts to real-life situations and that test required him only to produce square roots of numbers, he would probably score very high. But the test wouldn't be *valid* because it wouldn't have examined what it claimed to.

Here's another example. If we believe that reading requires *understanding* of what we've read and we give tests that measure letter identification or sounding out words from lists, some children could end up with a score that looks pretty good. However, that test would be invalid because it didn't really measure reading ability or reading growth. It didn't measure what it claimed to assess. It would reflect something similar to the *Rain Man effect*—the ability to recall isolated facts or perform isolated skills with little or no ability to apply them.

The empty, low-level facts that children "learn" to satisfy the tests are in many ways analogous to Raymond's skills. They are *basic*. And they are useless without the ability to apply them strategically. A heavy focus on testing instead of thinking and application actually encourages lower-level skills. As a matter of fact, there is a clear statistical link between relatively shallow, or basic, thinking and high scores on standardized tests.[24]

And don't forget that the federal government does not believe that all children are created equal. The children whose parents can afford to send them to private schools are exempt from the plague of testing that afflicts children in public schools. Is that fair? *If* standardizing children's performance is as important as the federal government claims, then why don't those standards apply to *all* children equally? Why aren't the children of the wealthy and those attending private schools labeled, sorted, and punished right along with the children of the poor and the middle class— those who traditionally attend public schools?

Let's keep in mind the question we asked some time back: Is it possible that rather than reforming public education, the federal government is seeking to eliminate it? Is it possible that instead of closing the gap between the children of the wealthy and the children of middle-class, working-class, and poor parents, the goal is to widen it by legislating unequal standards and expectations? To use the analogy that you applied to Chester Finn back in Section 2, is it possible that the buzzword of *accountability* is a clever manipulation by the foxes who are standing guard over the chicken coop?

Fallible Wizards: When Right Answers Are Wrong

So now, since the testing stakes are so high, you ought to have at least some assurance that if your children or your students are good little test takers and are having a good day, then they'll get their just rewards—a good score on the test—right? Wrong.

The test-making Wizards are fallible and they sometimes make mistakes on getting the answers right themselves, *and* the tests are sometimes incorrectly scored. Here's an example:

One of the major corporations that runs the testing industry is CTB/McGraw-Hill. In September 1999, the company admitted that it had incorrectly scored the reading and math tests of nearly ten thousand students in New York City. "The error made it look as if test scores had dropped precipitously from the year before."[25] As a result, through no fault of their own, thousands of third and sixth graders were sent to summer school. So taxpayers lost money and kids lost their summer.

Not only were children told they were failures and forced to spend their time in summer school and to receive "supplemental" tutoring with government-approved corporate programs, but as a result of the supposed failures, a number of school administrators were fired. Those are high stakes indeed based on an alarmingly fallible system. Thus, not only children tremble in the presence of such power; teachers and school administrators are held captive by testing, too. Their jobs and their reputations rest on forcing children into higher scores on more tests that measure how well they take the tests instead of how well they can apply truly important knowledge in real-life situations. And isn't that, after all, what we promise children schooling is all about?

"Oops! Sorry."

But the damage didn't stop there with the incorrect scoring that penalized so many children and teachers. The following June, the Board of Education in New York City accused the huge testing business of miscalculating the scores yet again. Remember this is but one example of errors made on standardized tests—in but *one* city—that changed lives. How many more errors have not been identified? How many more children are incorrectly labeled and punished as a result? All our eggs are in one basket that has a big hole in the middle of it. We need to ask why the accountability Wizards don't hold the test makers as responsible for errors as they do the test takers.

Other examples of kids who fell victim to errors in the CTB/ McGraw-Hill tests include students who couldn't graduate or were forced to repeat a grade because of errors in the construction or scoring of tests. When that happened on a large scale, the testing company essentially said, "Oops. Sorry." This is small consolation for the teachers and the schools that were publicly embarrassed or were fired and for those thousands of kids who were punished with summer school and were given the message that they were too stupid to pass to the next grade—and were held back. This is to say nothing of the millions of our tax dollars that were wasted. Testing is not free. It is *big* business. Make no mistake about it.

Don't forget that there is a degree of humiliation that goes beyond just the overt harm of a poor score. The scores of schools and teachers are published in newspapers with all the sensitivity of a public execution. Again, doesn't it strike you as odd that a multimillion-dollar testing industry that trades on accountability and right and wrong answers for *our* children shrugs off its own responsibility to get its own questions right and to score its own tests correctly with a casual "oh well"?

I agree with you. I've always hated those multiple-guess-type questions. But not all test questions are cut-and-dried, multiple-choice questions, are they? Don't some questions demand essay-type responses and assess deeper, more complex thinking skills?

Of course, the *obvious* problem with essay tests is that students are required to respond to, analyze, and perform the writing equivalent of biopsies on dissected specimens of mummified text that they have no interest in. Since these tests are timed, the pressure is enormous and students don't have the luxury of thinking, planning, and revising their answers. It is pretty much a one-shot, one-draft procedure—the antithesis of how good writing is accomplished. Just ask Stephen King or any journalist.[26]

But the *real* atrocity is how those essays are scored. In Alfie Kohn's seminal book *The Case Against Standardized Testing: Raising the Scores, Ruining the Schools* he notes that in many states, the essays children write on standardized tests are not scored by educators or even testing company Wizards. Instead, they are shipped off to a company "where low-paid temp workers spend no more than two or three minutes reading each one." One former "rent-a-scorer" told a reporter, "There were times I'd be reading a paper every ten seconds" and "[we] would only briefly scan papers before issuing a grade . . . I know this sounds bizarre but you could put a number on these things without actually reading the paper."[27]

There's more. These rent-a-scorers were offered cash bonuses that would kick in after they'd raced through their eight thousandth paper. And so it's obvious that the priority was not quality. Not validity. And certainly *not* personal attention to your child's or your students' essays. The priority was on quantity and of course money—*your* money—since *your* tax dollars pay for the tests and the scoring too.

But I read a newspaper article that said there is a body of core knowledge that all of us should know. That makes sense to me. Don't we need standardized tests to assess that knowledge?

OK. Let's look at the questions and the "core" knowledge that standardized tests supposedly assess. Who determines what, out of a *universe* of knowledge in history, literature, science, and mathematics, every educated U.S. citizen should know? A bunch of Wizards who work for a major corporate testing company sitting around a table decide—that's who.

 Not true.

There is nothing magical or absolute about what they figure is important for kids to know. If there were one North Star of Essential Knowledge, then all standardized tests would cover the same material and would have essentially the same questions, right? Well, they don't.

As a matter of fact, there is so much variation in what standardized tests cover that when schools switch from one testing company to another, the scores drop, because the questions are different than what the teachers and the children previously focused on.[28] If there were one magical body of essential knowledge floating around out there, then we'd see consistency between tests made by different companies, and we don't.

Just be sure you understand that my point is *not* that all children should be tested on the same content. My point is that the variations in content establish that the whole process is arbitrary and at the whim of the Wizards, who determine children's futures with a nod of their heads and a stroke of their pens. Once that "essential knowledge" is mandated, schools, teachers, and the way our kids are trained to think—and *what* they think—are controlled by the government and the publishers.

How Culturally Literate Are *You?*

As we have seen, everyone's list of what everyone *else* should know differs. In her book *One Size Fits Few: The Folly of Educational Standards*, Ohanian cites E. D. Hirsch, who decided he is the expert who should determine what everyone else should know. He wrote a book titled *Cultural Literacy: What Every American Needs to Know.*[29] Here, Ohanian gives us an example of how whimsical and esoteric core knowledge can be.

> What do you know about Leyden jars and when did you know it? How are your Mach numbers? Is your amicus in working order? [Can you] recognize such terms as covalent bonds, The Edict of Nantes non compos mentis, Plancks's constant, the Slough of Despond, and scrotum? . . . Oh, and Hirsch includes among his "must knows" the song, "La Cucaracha." Why is anybody's guess. (*viii*)

My hat is off to you if none of Hirsch's selection of core knowledge gave you pause. My educated guess, though, is that you scratched your head when you read that list. I know I did.

Double Standards or "How to Have Some Fun!"

If you're interested in a little challenge, here's an experiment for you to consider. Ask any of the legislators or standards-bearers who are so committed to labeling and testing our children to take those tests themselves. Many of us who are committed to revealing the threats and the folly of the testing movement have done just that. To my knowledge, not one has agreed to test his own essential knowledge on the same tests that he is selling to label our children. Or, try asking any school board members who think testing is the cure for all the ills of education to put themselves on the line by taking these tests **and having their scores made public.** My guess is that you will be met with silence. I'd be shocked if anyone took you up on it.

Owens did + didn't do too well.

Tentative Disclosure

The core knowledge that I cited as declared by Hirsch is not necessarily included in questions on standardized tests. I can't publish actual test questions because it's illegal to do so and those who do publicize actual content are prosecuted. The testing Wizards protect the questions with the same zeal as might be applied to any issue endangering our national security.

> The reasoning for keeping test questions secret goes like this:
>
> - These test questions represent *essential* knowledge for the youth of America.
> - If these test questions representing essential knowledge fall into the hands of parents and teachers, *then . . .*
> - teachers and parents will make sure that children can master this essential knowledge, and *then . . .*
> - more students would possess this essential knowledge and they would do better on our standardized tests, and *then . . .*
> - too few children would be left behind, and *then . . .*
> - we would have to find new averages and norms on our tests and that would be bad. *And* so . . .
> - We *must* keep essential knowledge top secret so only a privileged few can succeed.
> - If the *essential knowledge became common knowledge*, we couldn't sell schools and teachers our expensive test preparation books, and that would be *really* bad! And so . . .
> - we must make sure that essential knowledge for children remains top secret.

It appears that the Republican Party and the Bush administration are the ones wreaking this havoc on our schools. Is that what you're saying?

Yes and no. The increase in federal control and the whole testing and accountability movement started back with the Clinton administration. What makes the present political climate unique and what makes it so dangerous is that the control of the schools has been institutionalized and it is systemic. *And* it is coming from a political party that has traditionally denounced strong federal control. So we need to ask, "What's up here?"

So, this is not, strictly speaking, about President Bush or Chester Finn or any of the other politicians who control so much of our lives while giving us the illusion that they are working on our behalf. It is about *asking the right questions and the hard questions so that we don't give away our power and our rights as American citizens.* Remember the quote from Justice Jackson in Section 1?

It is not only our right to question the government and our leaders. It is our responsibility. It's our patriotic duty. And we need to keep asking those questions regardless of what political party is in power.

WHY MANY CHILDREN MUST BE LEFT BEHIND BY NCLB: HOW STANDARDIZED TESTS GET NORMED

As we've seen, standardized tests are all about comparing children to each other, and in any measure that makes comparisons, someone must be left behind. We've recognized some of the characteristics of standardized tests. Now we'll look at the norming procedure that makes a test standardized. It works like this: The testing companies administer the tests to large populations of children who are peers in age and grade and are within the range of "normal" in terms of their intellectual abilities. The children's scores are laid out along a kind of imaginary line that shows how many children achieved each score. Then the scores of all the children on each section of the test are added up. The sum is divided by the total number of children who took the test so that an *average*, or a *mean*, is determined.

If we draw a diagram or a curve showing the test scores, what we will see is that *because* the tests compare children and *because* a mean is found, half the children will be above the mean, but half the children *must* be below the mean. The procedure of establishing a baseline of performance that plays itself out along a predictable distribution with most scores lumped in the middle around the mean, and a fairly even tapering of middle to higher and middle to lower scores is called *norming*.

That ideal distribution is what we know as a *bell-shaped curve*. If too many children score too low, or if too many children score too high, then the bulge of the bell moves away from the middle and the distribution of scores is *skewed* toward one end or the other. When that happens, the testing company makes adjustments to make sure that most of the scores are in the middle. In other words, they recalibrate so that there are some "winners" at the high end and also some "losers" at the low end. As a matter of fact, in these competitive times we live in, even "average" is considered by many to be not good enough.

An example is the pressures and penalties of testing in Florida. There, third graders must achieve a score *above* the mean—*above* average at the fifty-first percentile—in order to pass to fourth grade. The most obvious problem is that even "average" children must fail. This absurd "standard" guarantees that *more than* 50 percent of the children *must* fail. But the more subtle problem is that on any standardized test, there is what's called a *statistical margin of error*. This means that there is a range—*rather than a precise score*—that is the true indicator of a level of performance. In Florida, the government is failing children based on scores that fall *within* this margin of error. Therefore, children are re-peating a grade or are suffering through summer "reading camps" or they're drilled in commercial supplemental programs, following scripted drills, when they are actually reading better than 50 percent of the children anyway. *And* they are being scored by a standard that even the testing companies don't approve of.

> In embracing standardized testing as the tool of scientific measurement, they have disregarded the testers' own cautions. Harcourt's Stanford 9 manual warns that a major "misuse of standardized achievement test scores is making promotion and retention decisions for individual students solely on the basis of these scores."[30]

In spring 2003, more than forty-three thousand children in Florida were not permitted to advance to fourth grade. That is nearly a quarter of all third graders in the state. These failures translate to successes for another big growth industry, for-profit education companies such as Sylvan Learning that our tax dollars now subsidize. Part of the NCLB choice that is no choice is that parents can "choose" to have their failing children tutored by government-approved companies. Sylvan is one of them. In the meantime, remedial services with proven results based on scientific, longitudinal studies, such as Reading Recovery, are excluded.[31]

The idea of choice for schools and in programs amounts to a myth. Recall Rod Paige's letter outlining what schools must do to receive funding. It all comes back to a choice that must be based on "scientifically proven" programs, a limited selection to say the least. It's like advertising a smorgasbord and when the hungry person enters the restaurant, presenting her with a choice of this potato or that potato. And teachers and schools don't find this out until they've taken the government at its word and spent hours writing Reading First grants—meeting the scientific criteria—only to be told that they must use a particular, government-chosen program.

For example, in New York City and Birmingham, Alabama, teachers spent hours of their own time laboring in good faith to meet Reading First requirements, only to be told—after the fact—that they had no choice in the selection of their supplemental provider. Voyager was imposed on them. The research for Voyager was conducted by Joe Torgesen, a favored researcher and grant recipient in Jeb Bush's state of Florida. Torgesen just happens to be a member of the Voyager design team.[32]

I'm going to make a statement here that I'd like you to keep in mind until we get to the way the government and corporations manipulated and misreported their own "scientific research." The definition of *science* now amounts to this: "If we approve of it, it's 'scientific.' If we don't, it's not." In other words, there is no set standard, no North Star or firm, objective definition of science. So the term *science* has become a convenient and very effective catchall term that means "Do this. And don't ask any questions."

But on the whole, children could show substantial improvement over time and then generally speaking, fewer and fewer would be behind. So I still don't understand why the standardized testing system makes sure some children lose out.

Look at it this way: Imagine a horse race with ten horses running. It's impossible that they will all come in first. It can't happen. Half of the horses will finish more slowly than the average time.

Even if we train those horses and they *all* do better than they did when they first got tested, only one can come in first and all the rest are left behind, and half *must* be below average. So, the average score moves up all right, *but* you cannot have more than half of *any* group be above average.

Take a look at the diagram in Figure 1 of a skewed distribution of scores. See that big hammer pounding the lump at the high end? That's the fist of the testing company's renorming to make sure too many children don't succeed and throw off the curve of the ideal winner-loser distribution of scores. If too many children manage to reach that high-end lump—then too bad for them—the tests will be renormed so there are enough losers to satisfy the bell-shaped curve. And incidentally, their teachers are pushed down with them. That sacred bell will not be unrung. It is a no-win situation for many schools, teachers, and students.

What's more, let's say a child is labeled "below average" or "at risk" in his own school or district. He can still be *above* the national average. There are so many loopty-loops going on behind the testing curtain that it is mind-boggling.

LABELING OUR PRESCHOOL CHILDREN

So . . . we've seen a shift from occasional standardized testing to a testing takeover. We've seen that the stakes are way higher than they were when we were in school and that the test-making Wizards make mistakes that don't hurt them—but can certainly hurt our children.

Now we'll look at yet another group of children the testing companies have targeted—preschool and kindergarten children. If a young child fails one of these tests, he can be labeled and treated as if he has a problem *before he's ever even started school* and has had a chance to adjust to the school environment.

As we will see later in this book, phonics has always been a profitable product for publishers. But now we have an old-new growth industry in education: *phonemic awareness* (PA). The false claim is that based on children's PA ability, the Wizards can predict how well they will be able to read in the future.

FIGURE 1 Bell-Shaped Curve *by Georgia Hedrick*

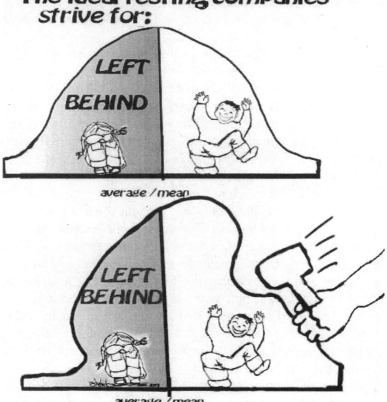

"When too many children improve, the normal curve is 'skewed' toward the high end . Then, testing companies 'renorm' so that the bulk of children's scores are pushed back to the middle to make sure that enough children are 'left behind'. "

What is phonemic awareness anyway? I've never even heard of it.

You are not alone if you've never heard of phonemic awareness. If you're over twenty, in all probability, you never received any direct training in it either. And yet—here you are, smart, successful, a good parent or teacher, and you're reading this book just fine.

So what is this "new" cure for the reading problems of children? Phonemic awareness is the ability to hear or say a word and break it into its individual components and/or blend the sounds together. It does not involve seeing a word or actual reading— only listening and speaking—so there is no reading involved.[33]

The tests that are given to preschool and kindergarten babies to decide their ability in PA go like this. A little child sits down in a strange setting with a strange person. That tester gives the child a series of tasks such as "Say 'butterfly.' Now say it without 'butter,'" and "Say 'split.' Now say it without the first sound."

Here's a little test for you. Try saying "split" without the first sound. Award-winning linguist and researcher Stephen Krashen notes that if *you* try this, you will probably picture the word in your head and then "delete" the first letter. Now imagine the confusion of a four- or five-year-old child being asked to do this and being labeled as "at risk" if she can't. *You* no doubt had to think pretty hard to do the sound segmenting yourself. Imagine a child being treated as if he were academically deficient based on tasks such as this before he even started school.

This would be almost funny if it weren't so serious. Perhaps the child is shy, or scared, or maybe just develops a little more slowly than other children and can't do this task. Stephen Krashen warns that the new growth industry of phonemic awareness training keeps getting pushed on children earlier and earlier in spite of extensive research findings that indicate that such training does *not* produce any lasting benefits and that ability in phonemic awareness can be acquired from reading. In other words, research suggests that PA can be a result of, rather than a cause or a valid predictor of, competent reading.[34]

At this rate, Krashen says, he wouldn't be surprised to see entrepreneurial researchers selling programs for prenatal PA training. While his quip is meant to be facetious, Krashen makes a serious point about the dangers of labeling and sorting children based on their ability to perform phonemic awareness tasks.

Incidentally, for the record here, I'm not opposed to pho
awareness, but I am opposed to labeling children as "a
based on this skill. And I am opposed to misrepresented research
that sells expensive phonemic awareness programs as the cure for
reading problems. As I said, more about this later.

A Story About My Son

My son, Chris, is eighteen months younger than my daughter,
Holly. When Holly started kindergarten, she could already read
and write. Then along came Chris, who had a speech defect and
was self-conscious about talking at all, even to us. He was frustrated, embarrassed, and upset when even we—his parents who
loved him—couldn't understand him.

When Chris started school, he didn't respond to teachers and
to the school setting the way his more outgoing older sister did.
He was shy and he was desperately afraid of making a mistake. In
kindergarten, his teacher—who meant well, I know—thought
she saw red flags and that maybe Chris had a learning disability
or was possibly even mentally retarded. She had him tested and it
was recommended that he be put into a special education class.

We refused to have Chris labeled as "retarded" and we took
him to a speech therapist outside of the school who was very
warm and who established a relationship with Chris over time.
When he finally tested Chris, we discovered that far from being mentally retarded and needing special education placement,
Chris' IQ put him in the gifted range and there was a less than
five-point difference between Chris' and Holly's IQs. This meant
that, based on the test, his score was well within the margin of
error, and so my children's IQs were virtually the same. Like so
many children, Chris just developed differently along a different
time line than other children. Not better, not worse, just different.

One of those who advocates labeling very young children
on their ability to segment sounds is Joseph Torgesen, who as
you'll recall is a member of the Voyager Learning design team.
We'll look at more of the "research"-financial-political links that
characterize Voyager and other programs later in the book.

I know that there are some extreme cases where a young child
has very definite physical or even emotional problems that need
special care and attention. Phonemic awareness is *not* one of
those special needs that cries out for remedial training, labeling,

and placement. It's not just ridiculous. It is tragic. And just coin-cidentally, of course, it's profitable for the remediation industry.

THE REPERCUSSIONS OF STANDARDIZED TESTING

Aside from the problems you cite concerning testing errors and scoring, generally speaking, doesn't testing help focus teaching energy toward important, common instructional goals and therefore elevate the caliber of students?

No. A large research study showed that after a period of time, students' performance does increase on the *specific* standardized test that students take, *but* student performance on other mea-sures of achievement consistently drops.[35] In fact, "twice as many states slipped against the national average on the SAT and the ACT as gained on it."[36]

One of the states that has been the most enamored of No Child Left Behind and serves as a model for standards, high-stakes testing, and, of course, accountability is California. It is also a model for failure. Despite spending "billions of dollars on school reform," despite implementing every piece of NCLB legislation including curriculum saturation by phonics-heavy programs such as the Open Court Reading series, despite the elimination of bilingual education with the promise that chil-dren's scores would improve in less than a year, despite high-stakes testing, despite a chorus of hallelujahs and hosannas of ac-countability, our children—and our teachers—were labeled as losers.

In fact, according to the latest Nation's Report Card by the NAEP (National Assessment of Educational Proficiency), "21% of fourth graders and 20% of eighth graders were proficient in reading last year, mirroring figures from 1992, according to the state-by-state report issued by the U.S. Department of Educa-tion."[37] And so it goes on the high-stakes No Child Left Behind fast track.

Researcher and educator David Berliner hypothesizes that the reason for the drops in other areas of achievement in schools that are heavily driven by high-stakes tests is that the teachers narrow their instruction to the content of the district's standardized tests because their jobs depend on student performance. The entire culture of the school changes during the time of test preparation, and all energy is focused on preparing students to take the particular upcoming test.[38]

Teaching the Tests

Last summer, I taught a teacher preparation class at California State University–Fresno. One of the course requirements was that our students spend time in classrooms with teachers and children. The local schools were holding six-week sessions so there should have been no problem. There was a big problem, though, because standardized tests consumed the time that those children should have spent learning.

Teaching in the school stopped for two weeks of test preparation and one entire week of actual testing. In other words, one half of that summer school session was dedicated to test taking and tests. Like the Hogwarts School of Wizardry in the fifth Harry Potter book, the schools transmuted into test preparation institutions instead of halls of learning.

Another atrocity is the fact that there is a long lag between the test taking and when the results are returned. Teachers don't get the results back until their students have already gone from their classes and it's too late to use those findings to help children—even if we assume that the test content is educationally valuable.

I'm starting to understand the dangers, the flaws, and the impact that testing has on the entire system and most importantly on children. But still, doesn't the promise or the threat, as it were, of upcoming tests inspire kids to work harder, especially if they haven't done well on those tests in the past?

Failure Inspires Success?

Now you've raised a question about yet another urban legend—the myth that failure inspires effort.

Can you remember how you felt when you were about to be tested? Do you recall the almost unbearable anxiety, the sweaty, trembling hands, and the looming fear of failure? Do you remember going home and second-guessing the answers you'd put down, and do you remember beating yourself up for mistakes you made?

And do you remember ever feeling embarrassed and "less than" because of your performance on a test? I do.

The pressure, the *fear* of failure, and the *actual* failure may well do the opposite of raising performance, much less inspiring a love of learning—they cause students to react as any of us do. Students avoid the source of pain—in this case, school and academics.

The Failure of Failing Kids

We have more than one hundred years of evidence that consistently, irrefutably shows that retaining children or flunking them does not make them successful. It makes them ashamed, it makes them bitter, it places them in classes with children who are younger than they are, and it turns them into dropouts—but there is no evidence that it helps them academically, much less emotionally and socially. Reading Hall of Fame member Richard Allington reminds us that there is not a study you can find that says flunking a kid turns him into a better student. A student who can't read in the fourth grade can't read any better sitting in a third-grade classroom.

Let me ask you a question here: What was your favorite subject in school? Did you focus your energy on something you weren't good at and keep practicing at it until you'd mastered it by way of improving your character, or did you avoid what you'd failed at? If you were horrible at math, chances are you hated it and didn't set your sights on improving in it enough to become a CPA or a scientist. If you hated poetry, I doubt that you are now writing poetry in your spare time. Isn't it natural to gravitate toward what makes us feel good about ourselves? Furthermore, there's another fundamental flaw in the choplogic driving the high-stakes testing obsession: Does weighing the puppy more frequently give him an incentive to gain weight?

What you say about avoiding failure makes sense intuitively, but what are the facts? How do we know that failure turns kids off instead of inspiring greater effort?

Human Sacrifices

The fact is that in big "model" testing states such as California and Texas, the dropout rates have increased since the federal government mandated more and earlier testing. More students, particularly minorities, are dropping out in ninth grade because

[handwritten margin notes:] What about Adams 60??

What about P. Pollacco & Michael Crichton??

of the looming threat of testing and failure. Dropouts among students with disabilities skyrocketed from 7,600 in 1996 to 9,600 in 2001 (last available data). IEP diplomas (not a high school diploma!) increased by 27 percent in the same time period. For many young people, dropping out is not voluntary. Between 1998 and 2001, more than 160,000 children were "pushed out" of New York City schools.[39] Thus, these children are not just left behind—they are driven out of the picture altogether.

Here's yet another example of how we must listen to public officials and read news articles from a critical and even cynical perspective. The Houston schools, which were touted by then Governor, now President Bush to the extent that they have been facetiously labeled "the Texas Miracle," are now accused of Enron-type accounting in manipulating their data. After a state audit, the following "error" was reported: Houston reported a dropout rate of only 1.5 percent. The audit revealed that it is at least 40 percent.

All of these students, then, were not just left behind but were rendered invisible and not even worthy of mention by the Houston schools. Even though the Houston schools ranked near the bottom of the country's largest school districts, and three Texas schools are among the country's worst for the percentage of students who graduate high school, the legend of the Texas Miracle persists. In fact, our secretary of education, Rod Paige, defended the award Houston Schools received as the Best Urban School District in the United States.

Another example of Enron-like accounting is the hidden shedding of students in New York City schools.

> The city data make it impossible to determine just how many students are being pushed out, where they are going and what becomes of them. But experts who have examined the statistics and administrators of high school equivalency programs say that the number of "pushouts" seems to be growing, with students shunted out at ever-younger ages.
>
> *Those students represent the unintended consequence of the effort to hold schools accountable for raising standards: As students are being spurred to new levels of academic achievement and required to pass stringent Regents exams to get their high school diplomas,* many schools are trying to get rid of those who may tarnish the schools' statistics by failing to graduate on time. *Even though state law gives students the right to stay in high school*

until they are 21, many students are being counseled, or even forced, to leave long before then.

And yesterday, after declining to comment on the issue for two months, Chancellor Joel I. Klein conceded the point. "The problem of what's happening to the students is a tragedy," he said, *"It's not just a few instances, it's a real issue."* (Emphasis mine.)[40]

Fact: Since the focus on testing, standards, scientific methods, and accountability has intensified, dropout and forced-out rates have increased.

Therefore: Can't we reasonably assume that high stakes, high pressure, the threat of failure, and all the time wasted on test preparation are turnoffs rather than incentives for increasing numbers of students?

I see a lot of articles about New York, Texas, and California schools and I hate to admit this, but I just skip over them. What's happening in those states is pretty sad from what I can tell, but it doesn't have anything to do with me because I don't live there.

I used to feel the same way until I finally understood that big states are the leaders in educational policy. They have the most students. They are the states that the publishers target first and that get hit the hardest. They predict *our* future. If you skipped over that paragraph on Texas school failure because you don't live in Texas and you believe that the information here doesn't apply to your children or your school, consider this: President Bush and the secretary of education of this country have elevated Texas schools as a model for the rest of the country. In fact, Paige was the superintendent of Houston schools up until 2001. Therefore, the methods he implemented, including the use of Open Court Reading, are now reflected in Houston's performance. Use these methods and these programs and your school too will achieve this level of success. We all need to think about that.

Questions for Discussion: What price do we pay as a society for student dropouts? Where do kids who feel alienated from the school culture turn to find acceptance? How do feelings of stress, worthlessness, and anger play themselves out in the actions of young people in our American culture?

Section IV

A HARD LOOK AT STRESS AND COMPETITION

Overemphasis on the competitive system and premature specialization on the grounds of immediate usefulness kill the spirit on which all cultural life depends, specialized knowledge included.

—Albert Einstein, *New York Times*, 1952

Stress is a way of life. So is competition. My child might as well get used to it. I see the stress of testing as a way of preparing him for the stress he'll experience in the future. Don't you agree?

Hmmmmm . . . so let me understand you here. Stress is a way of life and children need to practice being stressed so they can be *less* stressed at some later date? Is that how it works for us? When you're stressed at work, do you come home and prepare for the next day by seeking out yet more stressful activities to build up your "stress muscles"? Or do you come home, try to clear your mind, turn off the reruns of the day's events, and tranquilize the squirrel that's reeling around like crazy in your head, doing the fandango across your brain? Don't you want to kick back with a beer, a glass of wine, or a cup of tea and watch TV or read? What awaits your child when he gets home from school? More homework. More busywork. More of the same grind, grind, grind, and no relief in sight.

56

Here's an interesting coincidence. *At the very moment I'm writing these words* on July 1, 2003, I have the *Today Show* on and they're repeating a broadcast from the nightly news on stress. In fact, I've just looked up the actual study so I can cite it. The research reconfirms other findings showing that the dangers of stress include increased rate of aging and reduced functioning of our immune systems because of a chemical our bodies secrete when we are under stress, particularly when it is unrelieved. The worst kind of stress, according to the researchers, is caused when we feel that we have little or no control over our lives.[41]

Furthermore, the latest findings in brain research (to say nothing of our own experiences and common sense) prove that our brains need downtime—moments of quiet or changes in activity. When we experience extended, unrelieved periods of concentration without such logical—and humane—respites from stress, our brains make their own downtime. They shut off because if they don't, emotional problems can result. It's the brain's way of protecting us from ourselves.[42]

We are adults and we have problems finding quiet time—little pockets of peace—when we can stop to replenish our mental and physical resources. How much more difficult is it for children, who have even less control over their lives than we do to deal with the competition, the debilitating leaching of self-esteem that comes from being labeled as "less than," and the soul-murdering fear of letting **you** down that results from the increased pressures, the increased academic demands, and the ever present threat of failure that is being imposed on them?

I see your point. I know that my child dreads school, but I didn't realize that she's being driven to the extent that she is. But isn't competition healthy and isn't it one of the fundamental tenets of the free enterprise system? My child needs to learn to compete. Wouldn't you agree?

It's not my business to agree or disagree. You yourself need to decide if and when a line's been crossed and competition stops being healthy and starts poisoning your child's life. What we need to remember, though, is that NCLB is based on *forcing* competition among schools, teachers, and children. To me, that's crossing the line of local control. And as we've seen, it is based on prejudicial standards and a fallible system, and by its very design, leaves children behind. In other words, the sorting and labeling of our children doesn't fall into the same category as a good-natured game of Parcheesi™.

In addition to the competition that permeates our society right down to our humor, kids are now forced onto a ruthlessly competitive fast track and are driven to fight for their survival in a ruthlessly competitive arena—our schools.

But maybe the decisions for increased testing and competition among schools and children are well-intentioned and the people making the decisions have the best interests of children in mind.

First, I don't agree that the school "reform" initiatives are well-intentioned at all, as you'll see when you come to the section of the book on the financial conflicts of interest that drive current politics. Let's just pretend, though, that the Wizards who are pushing buttons behind the curtain of school reform really do believe that stress, competition, and increasing the standards helps all children strive for excellence. If those are the values that the Wizards want to impose on their own children, I think it's sad but it's none of my business. What *is* my business, though, is that those entrepreneurial politicians and test publishers are imposing *their* values on *our* children. That is un-American. It is also illegal and runs counter to the law of local control that specifically prohibits such interference in the schools.

I understand some of the points you make and I have heard myself preaching kindness to my child while at the same time urging him to win, win, win and I've felt twinges of discomfort. I don't get the part about humor, though. How can humor be competitive?

I was puzzled too when my daughter made an observation about competitive humor. Holly pointed out that much of what we laugh at as Americans is based on insults and put-downs. The response of the victim is to come back with a retaliatory insult, thus escalating the level of nastiness. Holly reminded me that the elevation of one person or group *at the expense of another* is in fact a form of competition. And so, Holly told me, our humor in America, unlike that of Nepal—her husband's country—is competitive.

I'll use an example of a popular television show that illustrates Holly's point. In case you've never seen it, *Everybody Loves Raymond* is about Raymond, his wife, Deborah, and their three young children, who live directly across the street from Raymond's intrusive, meddling parents. While Raymond's mother is rather insidiously controlling, the father openly insults and demeans not only his wife but Raymond and his brother as well.

What bothers me isn't so much that the father is nasty, because his sons react realistically and are hurt and struggle to maintain some measure of self-esteem after what most of us would characterize as a lifetime of ego-murdering belittlement— if not out-and-out emotional abuse. It could serve as a lesson for how *not* to treat others, especially because we like Raymond and his brother.

What bothers me is the reaction of the audience to the father's verbal and emotional abuse of his children. The audience doesn't gasp. We don't hear a collective "tsk" or a stunned silence when the father insults his wife and children. Instead, the audience laughs. Furthermore, I believe those lines are written to elicit those laughs. And so in a way, the audience, and all of us who laugh along—including any children who watch what most critics would characterize as a family show—become accomplices in the father's emotional damaging of his children.

Oh, lighten up already. It's just a sitcom. You're making a big deal about nothing.

Let's just think a minute, before you decide. That sort of competitive nastiness in the form of insults and put-downs is not isolated to a single TV show, and let's face it, children and adults watch a lot of television. We hear a lot about the impact of violent movies and video games on children. Isn't it reasonable to question the impact and the message of humor as well?

The success of such sitcoms and the laughter from the audience—and maybe our laughter, too—at meanness and put-downs establish a model for children and, in doing so, validates the behavior that precipitated the laughs. It tells them that it's not just

OK, but that it's funny to ridicule others. If you don't believe me, spend a little time on a playground and with a group of kids and you'll see that same sort of demeaning nastiness—the emotional and physical bullying—played out in real life with *real* victims over and over again.

If you're still thinking my point about humor is much ado about nothing, then think back to your own experiences in schools. You remember grade school and high school. I'll be you can recall not just the physical bullies but the pervasive nastiness of the popular kids to those who are labeled as "less than" for whatever reason—whether physical or academic or just some poor kid who doesn't get it and dares to be different. I'd be willing to bet that someone—at some time—in your school career thought it was funny to tease you or to exclude you and that if that happened, the hurt is still there. So that kind of competitive nastiness is not trivial. And it is not funny either.

Just look and listen and I think you'll be surprised at just how pervasive unhealthy competition has become in our culture. As your homework (should you choose to participate), just sit and watch three sitcoms tonight. Make a list of what got laughs. In one column place the put-downs and the insults. In the other, put any other kind of humor—anything that does not sacrifice a character. If you have more items in the second column, I'll be amazed and I hope you'll send me your list! My email address is on the back of the book.

It's also reasonable to ask questions about the messages in other popular genres in entertainment. What is the moral message of reality shows such as *Survivor,* in which the goal is to cheat, lie, manipulate, and eliminate fellow contestants? Isn't much of the appeal of the top-rated *American Idol* just watching Simon humiliate and demean the contestants? So appealing is that level of nastiness that a poll identified Simon as one of the sexiest men in America.

Aren't we also preoccupied if not obsessed with ranking? There are endless lists of "top 10" and "worst," ranging from *People* magazine's list of most beautiful people, to the worst-dressed lists, who's in and who's out, and the lists go on and on and on. What are the values that are inherent in such rankings? What is the message with which we and our children are relentlessly bombarded?

What I'm saying here is that sorting and labeling and elevating ourselves at the expense of others are seamlessly woven in the fabric of our culture from the television shows we watch, to the video games our kids play, to the way our children and teenagers treat each other, to the attitude of slugging it out and beating the other guy by doing whatever it takes in business, in sports, and even in our personal and sexual relationships as adults.

And increased pressures and competition in schools start children on that road younger and younger. They can't succeed except at the expense of someone else, and teachers and districts can't hope for success unless someone else loses. It's all of a piece, and that competition—that culture of winning by putting down the other guy—has escalated until schools are feeding into it *at the same time* that we all preach "values" and "kindness" and "character."

At best, we as a society send kids mixed messages. At worst, we must look like a bunch of hypocrites to any young person who stops to think about it.

It's hard to argue with the points you've made and it leaves me with some hard decisions. What can I do to protect my child from those unhealthy messages and influences and try to reconcile some semblance of balance between my religious beliefs and the competition that, as you say, is everywhere?

First, we all need to clarify our values in our own minds. Make sure you know what it is that you believe in. Then, fight for those beliefs. In the box on page 62 are some hard questions for discussion that might help you look at competition across our society as a possible challenge to your moral and ethical beliefs. We need to recognize these hard questions before we can clarify and model our own values for children who look to us for answers.

I'd be interested in any reactions you have to these questions, or any viable options for addressing the challenges. Sincerely, I want to know what you think about it. I'd also be interested in any questions you raised yourself that I haven't included here.

It's important, too, to include your children or your students in this process. Talk to them. Listen to them. Discuss the pressures of school and guide them through it. Don't add to that stress.

Questions for Discussion

- How do we reconcile the concept of competition, which by its very definition is predicated on being better than, with the ethical and moral values of our personal religious or societal beliefs, which are often based on helping each other and on personal sacrifice?
- When does the principle of free enterprise cross the line and become a system of exploitation and greed as we saw with Enron? And who lost? The CEOs, who protected their pensions and their futures, or the little guys, who believed the propaganda and invested in the company?
- What is an appropriate ethical—and balanced—role for business in society?
- Can we entrust our children to the care of for-profit corporations in place of a public trust?
- Should schools be about competitive corporate values? If so, who do you suppose will win that competition? The corporate executives or the children in their care?
- Has the quest for excellence we associate with sports degraded into dirty business?
- Why do so many students cheat? What values are being played out when they do? In other words, which values win? The value of competition or the ethical and moral principles that we profess to value as a society?
- If there are contradictions and a blurring or even a slippage of values, then what message are we giving our children about who we are and what we want them to be?
- If you believe in transmitting values to children, then which values will you preach? "Win" or "Help others"? Either value in its purest form excludes the other. So how do we handle that contradiction?
- Albert Einstein made the following observation. What does it say about the conflicting messages our society may give children?

> Darwin's theory of the struggle for existence and the selectivity connected with it has by many people been cited as authorization of the encouragement of the spirit of competition. *Some people also in such a way have tried to prove pseudoscientifically the necessity of the destructive economic struggle of competition between individuals. But this is wrong, because man owes his strength in the struggle for existence to the fact that he is a socially living animal.* (Emphasis mine.)
>
> Albert Einstein, address at a celebration
> of the tercentenary of higher education
> in America, Albany, New York, 1936

The best way to do that is to let children know your love and your support are not contingent on performance on a test, in school, or in sports. Beware also of praising children. If children recognize that they please you by doing well, they will also sense that you're disappointed when they don't. That hurts. Start noting competition in our society and comment on it. Draw your child or your students into the discussion.

When you watch a TV show that is based on meanness and put-downs, don't laugh. Comment on how sad it is that people treat each other that way and see what your children think about it. We can't totally protect children from meanness and bullying, but we *can* help them recognize it, question it, and maybe even avoid the temptation to succumb to it.

Just recently, Fred Rogers, affectionately known to millions of us as Mr. Rogers, died. Shortly before his death he gave a commencement address that is a poignant reminder of the value of friendship and kindness as opposed to competition and winning at any cost. The children who were running the race in the story that follows are those who are left behind in this society of standards and high scores. This does not diminish their value as human beings. In fact, there is a lesson here for all of us who place so much value on winning.

I wonder if you've heard what happened at the Seattle Special Olympics a few years ago? For the 100-yard dash, there were nine contestants, all of them so-called physically or mentally disabled. All nine of them assembled at the starting line, and, at the sound of the gun they took off—but one little boy stumbled and fell and hurt his knee and began to cry.

The other eight children heard the boy crying. They slowed down, turned around, saw the boy, and ran back to him—every one of them ran back to him. One little girl with Down's syndrome bent down and kissed the boy and said, "This will make it better." The little boy got up, and he and the rest of the runners linked their arms together and joyfully walked to the finish line. They all finished the race at the same time. And when they did, everyone in the stadium stood up and clapped and whistled and cheered for a long long time.

People who were there are still telling the story with obvious delight. And you know why? Because deep down we know that what matters in this life is much more than winning for ourselves. What really matters is helping others win, too, even if it means slowing down and changing our course now and then.
  —Fred Rogers, Middlebury College Commencement, 2001[43]

One more quick point here, which is, in fact, the reason I wrote this section. Yes, I wanted us to think about competition and stress as they relate to our professed values. But more than that, I hope that even if we can't turn back the damage of school reforms, we can at least be aware of the mixed messages our kids are receiving and we can help them deal with stress. Recall the study on stress that I began this section with? One of the major points it makes is that it's unhealthy and dangerous for anyone to feel out of control for long periods of time. Talking honestly with a supportive adult is a way of addressing, processing, and even relieving pent-up emotions and anger for our children. Even if we can't fix the system, that is something we *can* do.

I agree that I need to become more politically aware and more actively involved in what happens behind the scenes in education. But, I work. I'm very busy. I don't have time for all that reading and discussing and political involvement. I'm a teacher as well as a parent, and our days at school are crammed full of mandated activities. And at home, we're all busy—each with our own "homework."

Please go back and read the paragraph about how we all need to identify and clarify our own values before we can establish our priorities. You can't help children shape their own beliefs if you yourself don't know what you stand for and are willing to protect. How much do those values mean to you? To what extent are your beliefs based on an informed examination of issues rather than on political or media buzzwords and clichés? In other words, are your values your own—or are they someone else's because staying informed and looking beneath the surface takes a lot of time? Once you've answered that question honestly, then you have assumed the responsibility of taking the time to advocate for those principles even if it *does* take time. Again, *what is it that you value?*

You wouldn't trust a repair person or home decorator alone in your home without your presence to supervise and to protect your valuables, would you? Why would you even consider handing your child over to virtual strangers, walking away, and hoping for the best? If you don't advocate for your child and for the children in your classrooms, who trust you to protect them, who will?

Both my parents were first-generation Americans and neither of them spoke English before entering kindergarten, and yet both had a keen, very refined sense of what it means to be an American. They didn't just preach their values. They lived them. When I was in school, my parents made time for PTA meetings and for teacher conferences, and they communicated with my teachers.

My parents stayed informed. They read the newspapers every day and they never just accepted that what they read in the paper was true. My mother in particular wrote letters to the editors about important local and national issues on a regular basis and I can remember helping her write those letters when I was only eight or nine years old. She made me a part of her literate, informed approach to life.

As a child, I took my parents' activism pretty much for granted, although I suppose I was pleased in some vague way. Today, though, I see how truly amazing my parents were. They set a model for informed advocacy and those actions helped to shape me way more than just preaching or words ever could. They always stood up for me and for what was right, and they taught me to do the same. That is a gift. It's a gift you can give your child, too. And as a teacher, it is one of the most important lessons you can ever teach.

LOOKING AT LEARNING

We've briefly discussed the fact that teachers must now devote excessive time to test preparation at the expense of teaching and that consequently, they are forced to focus on the narrow range of knowledge that the tests cover instead of a panorama of ideas and critical issues. We also saw evidence that such knowledge often involves basic, low-level thinking so that student "learning" becomes little more than the accumulation of facts that are useless without the ability to apply them—similar to the skills Raymond possessed but couldn't apply in the movie *Rain Man*. To fully understand schools and the harmful effect that current school "reform" has on the learning process, we need to look at how it is that we learn so we can then decide on the most effective teaching methods and materials. Or as Seymour Sarason asks, "What do you mean by learning?" (2004).

Section V

BOTTOM-UP TEACHING, METHODS, MATERIALS, AND RESEARCH

*It is not enough to teach man a specialty.
Through it he may become a kind of useful
machine but not a harmoniously developed
personality. It is essential that students acquire
an understanding of—and a lively feeling for—
human values. He must acquire a vivid sense of
the beautiful and of the morally good.
Otherwise he—with his specialized
knowledge—more closely resembles a well-
trained dog than a harmoniously developed
person.*

Albert Einstein, *New York Times*, 1952

*I always thought the meaning of **learning** was pretty obvious.
So I'm confused by all the fuss about the so-called reading
wars. What is there to even argue about?*

In this section, I've highlighted key vocabulary. Although educators and researchers have traditionally focused the wars on how
to teach reading, and most particularly on the role of phonics in
reading instruction, the real issue—the underlying conflict at the
heart of the battle that's raged for decades—is opposing views of
how we learn and consequently *how to teach most effectively*. So
the debate, or the wars as it were, extends to math, science, so-

cial studies, and all academic subjects, as a matter of fact. Therefore, it's more accurate to describe the conflict as "The Teaching-
Learning Wars."

The two extremes in the wars are sometimes characterized as
bottom-up, or *skills-first*, approaches, as opposed to *top-down*, or
meaning-first, views of how we learn. Certainly, when teachers
are permitted to make their own decisions about how to teach,
they may at times combine approaches and teach along a continuum and change their methods according to children's needs.
However, as we've seen, the right of teachers to make decisions,
including the option to choose their own materials and methods,
has been usurped by federal mandates in the name of educational
"reform." The methods that the federal government mandates
are at an extreme end of the teaching-learning continuum—a
bottom-up or basic-skills method.

In order to understand the impact these very different views of
teaching and learning have on children's mental and social development, we need to carefully examine these two approaches.
And so first, we'll look at the materials and the methods that
characterize them. Next, I'll give you a picture of two classrooms
in which the respective philosophies play out and discuss the
pros and cons of each of the approaches. We'll look at the research and relate it to your own experiences so that you can
come to your own conclusions and determine what teaching
methods and materials best reflect your own philosophy based on
how *you* yourself learn. In this section, I've highlighted many
questions for discussion for university classes or teachers and
parents.

Finally, we'll see whether the bottom-up teaching methods
the federal government is mandating for schools support—or discourage—deeper, higher-level thinking and learning and what
that means for our children. I'll focus here primarily on beginning reading instruction because that's the arena that seems to
generate the most rancorous controversy.

SKILLS-FIRST, OR BOTTOM-UP, VIEW OF TEACHING/LEARNING

The general procedures in bottom-up classrooms are probably
very familiar to you since it is the prevailing form of instruction
and has been since schooling began. Bottom-up classrooms re-

semble what we routinely see when schools are portrayed in movies or even in television commercials. Draw a picture of a schoolroom and there's an excellent chance that without even thinking, you've arranged it like this:

We see the teacher at the front of the room asking questions while the students are generally seatbound, sit in their straight rows, raise their hands, read aloud from textbooks, and answer questions. Students are responders, rather than initiators. Students may be seated at tables in groups, but the group work is teacher-controlled. Because of the respective roles of teacher and student, bottom-up classes are sometimes referred to as *teacher-centered* as opposed to *student-centered* or *constructivist* because the student's role in bottom-up classes is generally passive—that of a responder rather than an active initiator of questions and ideas.

Here's an overview of the philosophical beliefs behind bottom-up teaching as they relate to practice. Following this description, we'll look at how commercial materials control the teaching and learning and consequently the respective roles of teachers and students.

The Bottom Line on Bottom-Up Teaching

- Bottom-up instruction usually begins with the teaching and practice of *basic* skills, the building blocks—the pieces of print. Therefore, this method of teaching is referred to as bottom-up because the skills are taught sequentially from the bottom of the learning curve—the part, the piece, the letter, or the basic fact. It then proceeds upward to comprehension or application. Much of such traditional instruction is focused on facts and memorization.
- Proponents of bottom-up, skills-based instruction believe that comprehension and application to real-life situations will happen because the skills have been mastered. When comprehension is addressed, it too is usually taught separately from the skills that led up to it. Comprehension is also segmented into pieces (such as *inference* and *cause and effect*) that are taught directly and often separately from each other.

• In bottom-up instruction, often a lot of emphasis is placed on how fast the children read. The assumption is that *oral fluency* (the *speed* and accuracy of word recognition as well as correct intonation—sometimes referred to as *prosody*) helps comprehension. Bottom-up proponents believe that children who read quickly—and without error—can understand what they read. Many teachers who use a bottom-up approach test the children frequently on timed fluency tests to assess and encourage fast, accurate reading.

In the upper grades, the bottom-up, skills-focus sequence works in the same order—skills first, application later—but the skills may be more advanced than in the earlier grades. A teacher might, for example, explain a grammar skill such as providing the definition of a noun. Then the students practice nouns by circling all the nouns on a worksheet. Or a student might circle the subjects and the predicates in a sentence or practice putting apostrophes in words on a worksheet. You are probably very familiar with this method because it has been the traditional, most common method of teaching.

Bottom-Up Math

As I mentioned before, the debate over opposing philosophies and even bottom-up versus top-down teaching applies to math as well as to reading instruction. In this discipline, the sequence and procedures are basically the same as they are for bottom-up reading instruction. The teacher explains a mathematical skill, such as addition. The children practice that particular skill on worksheets or flash cards, in class and as homework. Then the teacher moves on to another skill, such as subtraction, multiplication, or division. Often, children are given timed tests to see how fast they can do basic math tasks such as addition, subtraction, and multiplication. These timed tests emphasizing speed and accuracy are roughly parallel to timed fluency tests for reading.

Bottom-Up Social Studies and Science

Children read through social studies or science chapters in textbooks. The focus is on facts, dates, and in science, memorizing formulas. The students complete worksheets or answer comprehension questions on the facts in the chapter and then are tested on how well they've memorized the facts.

Bottom-Up Reading Materials and Methods: Basal Readers

The materials and the teaching methods for bottom-up instruction are closely related. In fact, it *is* now the commercially produced reading series that control the reading curriculum in bottom-up classrooms rather than the teacher, since the federal government has taken over the schools. These reading materials are probably very familiar to you. They're called *basal readers*, *basals*, or sometimes *anthologies*, because they contain *collections of stories* or informational articles on which children apply their reading skills.

These basal series include *teacher manuals* with specific, very detailed directions for teachers to follow. The teacher moves through the sequence of instructions and covers the material along the time line outlined in the manual. The layout and some of the specifics vary from one commercial basal series to another, but we can identify certain general characteristics.

Basal Stories

Often, the beginning stories in the basals often rely on a *controlled vocabulary*—words that focus on the particular skill and are used repeatedly in stories so that children have many opportunities to practice and learn the skill or the word. For example, the controlled story vocabulary may focus on a phonics sound such as short *a*. The term *phonics* refers to the connection between a letter or group of letters and the sounds that it makes.

One of the main principles of bottom-up instruction is that children must have phonics skills in order to be competent readers and these skills must come *before* children can read instead of *as children are reading and writing*, which is how phonics is taught in the opposing top-down method. And so in bottom-up instruction, the teacher, for example, may introduce a skill such as short *a* as the sound we hear in the word *apple*. Next, the children practice identifying the sound on worksheets by writing *a* in the blanks on worksheets (c__t). Then they might read a story using *decodable text*. To qualify as decodable, *80 to 90 percent of the words must follow the rule and use the sound being taught.*[44] A typi-

cal story using vocabulary that is controlled—and decodable—
might read something like this:

> The fat cat sat.
> The fat cat sat on Rat.
> Rat is sad.
> The cat is bad.
> The cat is fat and bad.
> Bad cat.
> Sad Rat.

Currently, decodable text is a characteristic of government
mandated basals for beginning readers. However, a program
called *Language!* that uses decodable text is now being recommended for older students in junior high and high school, so
high school students are now reading stories such as "The Fat
Cat Sat."[45]

What Scientific Research Supports the Use of Decodable Text?

According to the government's own "comprehensive" research
on reading methods, the *Report of the National Reading Panel*
(NRP), there is not enough research on decodable text to support a recommendation for its use.[46]

As Richard Allington confirms, "there is no scientific evidence yet to support the use of decodable texts" (Allington and
McGill-Franzen 2001). Nevertheless, in California as well as
in an increasing number of schools nationwide, *Language!* is one
of the programs touting a scientific, government-sanctioned research base to support its use.

Perhaps coincidentally, Louisa Moats is the project director for
our government research agency the National Institute of Child
Health and Human Development. She is also Literacy Research
and Professional Development Director for the commercial program *Language!* It is distributed by McGraw-Hill Publishing,
which also publishes another approved program, Open Court
Reading.[47] In addition to her *Language!* connection, Moats is also
the project director for the government agency the National Institute of Child Health and Human Development (NICHD), the
agency that appointed the National Reading Panel, which re-

viewed and now recommends programs that are deemed to be "scientific" and acceptable to the federal government.

Question for Discussion: Given what you know about the interests and attitudes of older students, how might decodable stories such as those in *Language!* affect older students in terms of their self-confidence and their attitudes about reading and school?

In bottom-up basal reading series and in decodable texts, the phonics sounds and their rules are introduced one letter or sound at a time through a prescribed *sequence*. The sequence or the order of the sounds that is targeted differs from one series to another and there is no scientific evidence to support one sequence over another.

Questions for Discussion: What are the advantages and disadvantages of using decodable text for teaching reading? How might decodable text influence children's perceptions of the reading process? How might consistent use of decodable text impact their approach to comprehension over a period of time? How might it impact their general ability to identify words in real, more complex text?

Point: The Case for Decodable Text
- Decodable text drills children on letter sounds and gives them practice so they won't forget the rule or the sound.
- Decodable texts move from simpler to more complex combinations of sounds and phonics rules.
- Because the sounds in a decodable story are very regular and are easy to sound out, such controlled vocabulary allows children (or high school students) to sound out words immediately so they can read a story early in the learning process.

Counterpoint: The Case Against Decodable Text
- Decodable text gives students the false impression that the English language consists of a sound system that is regular and predictable. It is not. Therefore, students may have problems making the transition from the false promise of decodable text to real reading and writing.

- Decodable text trains children to look at the ending pattern and to just add a first letter to that pattern. Mostly, they concentrate on the first letter only, since the pattern is a given. Once they're in this habit, they make *quicky substitutions* when they come to more complex, real text. They look at the first letter of a word and say any word that begins with that letter whether it makes sense or not.
- Decodable texts are boring. They are like tongue twisters and it's hard to follow, much less care about, the "story." Therefore, children get into the habit of *not* cross-checking to see if their quicky substitutions make any sense. Therefore, decodable text works against comprehension, because the stories are strained, contrived, and don't make sense.
- There is no research to support the use of decodable text.

One way to use decodable text sensibly and to find a common ground between the two extremes of the pros and cons is by introducing a pattern such as __*at* and having the children write their own silly sentences. In this way, children can construct their own sentences and there is no misrepresentation or pretense that the decodable assemblage of words is a true story.[48] And so a steady diet of sequential, decodable nonsense stories is avoided and children can still practice the target skill. Unfortunately, in many districts such a compromise is no longer possible because the teachers must adhere absolutely and rigidly to the teacher manual of the government-approved reading series.

Another Type of Controlled Vocabulary: Sight Words

Sometimes the target skill and the controlled vocabulary of basals may focus on what are called *sight words*. These are words that are the most commonly used in English, such as *the, once, there, is,* and that may not follow phonics rules and therefore can't necessarily be sounded out. For example, if the sight word *once* were written as it sounds, it would be spelled *yuns* or *wuns,* but it isn't, and so it must be recognized on sight. Children need a large bank of sight words in order to be competent readers. The term *sight words* also refers to *any* words that a reader can readily identify without hesitation. A story using a controlled vocabulary of common sight words repeats the same words over and over again much the same way that a decodable text uses a limited number of target sounds and repeats them throughout the story. A story using a controlled sight word vocabulary of *Mr.*, *Mrs.*, *walks*, *and*, and *too* might read:

> Mr. White walks. [Note: *Walks* and *white* are sight words, as are many color words.]
> Mrs. White walks too.
> Mr. and Mrs. White walk and walk.

Questions for Discussion: How may stories using controlled vocabulary or decodable text affect the quality of literature? How might the quality of the stories affect students' motivation to read and their perceptions of the purpose of reading? How might consistent reading of such controlled stories affect students' ability to think and to comprehend what they read?

Whether the teaching focus of a lesson is on sight words or on letters or letter sounds, the hallmark of bottom-up teaching is that it begins with the skill, followed by practice of the skill, then practice in sentences, and finally practice of the skill by reading a story. Imagine a triangle standing on its head with the letter or skill at the point and comprehension at the top (see Figure 2).

FIGURE 2 Bottom-Up Skills Chart

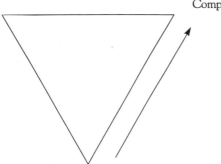

Comprehension or meaning is taught last

Skill is taught first

Other Materials for Sale

Other materials that the districts purchase in addition to the reading books and teacher manuals are no doubt also familiar to you. The children practice skills such as letter sounds (*phonics*) on *worksheets* and in *workbooks* that districts also buy from the publisher. These are also sometimes referred to as *consumable* materials because they must be repurchased regularly as the children use them.

Sometimes the basal reading books do include real stories by popular children's authors. Frequently though, the stories have been *edited* or *abridged* so that they can fit into the basal texts. Sometimes a single chapter cut from a popular children's book is included. Obviously an entire book can't fit into an anthology, and so children practice their reading skills on an excerpt that may not include the beginning or the middle or the end of a given story or book.

Question for Discussion: How might reading an edited story or requiring children to read only one chapter of a popular book for young people affect the quality of the literature as well as students' attitudes toward reading?

Bottom-Up Comprehension

The final step, the last rung on the teaching ladder for bottom-up instruction, is *comprehension*. Again, the practice component of this skill usually relies on worksheets or questions the teachers ask the children on the text they have just read. For example, in response to the samples of controlled text that I provided earlier, the children might answer questions such as "Who sat on the rat?" or "Who walks?" respectively.

As with the basic phonics or word skills, bottom-up comprehension is often divided into separate components. These might include comprehension skills such as requiring children to look for details in a story by answering questions like "Who sat?" and "Who walks?" Or the worksheet questions might require children to make *inferences*—reasonable assumptions about unstated ideas in a story, such as "Why was the cat fat?" Answer: "Maybe he ate too much or he didn't get enough exercise other than sitting on rats." Or, one piece of comprehension instruction might include *cause-and-effect* questions such as "Why was the rat sad?" Answer: "Because the cat sat on him."

In terms of allotment of instructional time as well as the nature of the stories in the texts, the goal of bottom-up reading instruction is on teaching skills and skills practice rather than on independent reading or on the literary value of the stories in the books.

Literature Supplements for Sale

In addition to the basal readers, districts can purchase accompanying books of popular children's or adolescent literature. These books are also taught through the prescribed procedures listed in the teacher manual and are usually used with worksheets, workbooks, and other skills and comprehension exercises.

Point: The Case for Worksheets

- They allow the teacher to focus on a particular skill and provide practice for children.
- They are easy to assess.
- They keep students busy so that the teacher is freed up to work with small groups.

Counterpoint: The Case Against Worksheets

- They're boring. They are the definition of *busywork*.
- They don't teach. They assess. To complete them, the students need to already know the skill that's required or they won't be able to fill in the blanks.
- Worksheets require low-level basic skills instead of high-level, creative thinking.
- Frequently, students don't need to think at all in order to complete worksheets. They quickly tune into the worksheet format and can often complete the skill pattern that's required without thinking.
- Research shows that children do not transfer isolated skills to real literacy. Filling in a blank is far different than the way a skill is used in real reading and writing.
- Worksheets are very expensive. The money wasted on them could be used on books and libraries.

Questions for Discussion: What experiences have you had with worksheets? Did you find yourself putting effort into completing them, thinking hard and creatively, or did you tend to routinely and rather thoughtlessly race through them to get them out of the way? Why did you react as you did?

Point: The Case for Basal Readers

• Teachers need a structure to work from.
• Teachers don't have the ability to make decisions about what they teach. Furthermore, they don't want to make decisions on their own. They want to be told what to do.[49]
• Children need structure too.
• Basic skills such as phonics must be taught sequentially, in a prescribed order.
• Although children learn and practice skills in isolated drills separate from real stories, they will transfer those skills to authentic text once they've achieved mastery.
• The curriculum needs to be standardized so all teachers at a grade level are teaching the same material at the same time. Basals help ensure standardization of teaching and learning.
• Because teaching is controlled by the basal reading series, teachers can be replaced by graduates of alternative commercial teacher training programs. These alternative teachers can be hired for less money and less costly fringe benefits than teachers who have completed rigorous training at universities.

Counterpoint: The Argument Against Basal Readers

• Teachers are intelligent, capable professionals who can and should make instructional decisions. They should be more than classroom managers, paper graders, and test givers.
• Teachers want to individualize classroom instruction because they realize children are all unique and they develop along different time lines. One size fits few. A standardized curriculum doesn't work because kids can't be homogenized and it's silly to think they can.
• There is no research to support the idea of an optimum sequence of skills. In fact, the sequence varies among reading series.
• The controlled vocabulary in basal reading series makes the stories about the words or the skill instead of about the story. The stories are boring and as a result, children think reading is boring.
• The format of the basals is divorced from the reality of how we read. As adults, we read books, not basals. Edited or

abridged stories lack the heart and flavor of the original and the author's art.

- When we seek out sources for information, we don't turn to a basal. We use a variety of sources. Therefore, not only the stories but the informational articles included in basals are artificial and are divorced from authentic application.
- Many children don't transfer skills learned in isolation to authentic application.
- It is dishonest to preach that reading is fun and then present a "cat sat" decodable story. It's even more dishonest to try to generate enthusiasm for such "stories" by pretending they are interesting or meaningful.
- Children need structure, but they must be motivated and engaged in the learning process or they'll tune out or drop out or just go through the motions instead of becoming active thinkers and learners.
- Basals are expensive. In times of budget deficits, it's cheaper and smarter to buy a variety of real books for children to read.
- Teaching is an art *and* a science. Teaching is a calling as well as a profession and teachers need more than just a basic knowledge of basic subject matter. They need to understand how children develop and learn. While a basal can provide ideas and support, especially for beginning teachers, the reading series used should not dictate the curriculum.

Objections to basal reading series have persisted for decades.[50] The debate is now more heated than ever because the choice of whether or not to use basals is no longer in the hands of teachers or even districts. As the federal government exerts its control, the selection of reading series from which districts can choose is extremely limited and must be approved by government experts if schools are to receive funds through federal Reading First grants.[51]

Questions for Discussion: Is there a place in reading instruction for basal readers? Is the mandating of scripted programs at all grade levels redefining what it means to be a teacher? Should teachers be decision makers and have the right to make decisions about children? If they don't, who is deciding school-level policy and materials? Is this shift to outside control good or bad?

We'll now look at one of the most widely used and controversial reading series, Open Court Reading by McGraw-Hill. It's controversial because it's widely used, its publisher has links to the Bush administration that many find to be questionable, and its effectiveness is highly debatable. Furthermore, the publisher of Open Court carries a big stick and its clout is far-reaching.

Section VI

GOVERNMENT-APPROVED PROGRAMS, METHODS, AND THE RESEARCH CLAIMS

GOVERNMENT-APPROVED READING PROGRAMS

One of the reading programs favored by the federal government is Open Court Reading, published by McGraw-Hill. In California, for example, the law mandates a selection of five reading series from which districts can choose. However, in spite of the law, the State Board of Education provides only two choices, one of which is Open Court. The other is Houghton Mifflin's Reading Program. Open Court is used widely across the country as well as in California *because* it is government-approved. Although the federal secretary of education claims there is no list of federally approved reading programs, districts don't receive federal monies for Reading First grants unless they use a *"scientifically approved core reading program,"* and Open Court is the hands-down favorite with the Reading First panels of experts.

And so we see the same doublespeak that has twisted the law of local control into a pretzel of federal control: Schools **can refuse** to use a government-approved reading program, but if they do so, they don't receive funding. And so the *choice* is but an illusion. As I said previously, rhetoric promises a smorgasbord that amounts to a choice of this potato or that potato. One of those potatoes is Open Court Reading.

As a matter of fact, the choice of reading programs is so narrow and the governmental control is so tight that when New York City schools chose to adopt Month-by-Month Phonics as their reading program because it was far less expensive than Open Court, *and* met the government criteria for "scientific" reading methods, President Bush's reading advisor, Reid Lyon, objected in a letter to the *New York Times*. Such "recommendations" by President Bush's reading advisor appear to be in direct defiance of the law of local control prohibiting government employees from recommending materials, curriculum, or methods and from even reviewing them.

In addition to Reid Lyon's letter, three members of the government-sponsored National Reading Panel also signed a letter attacking New York City's proposed decision to adopt Month-by-Month Phonics (MM) instead of a "program with scientifically proven results." The letter states that schools selecting MM instead of an approved program are "not likely to qualify for federal funding" and reminds school officials that "some of us [the letter's authors] are serving on committees at the federal level involving the No Child Left Behind legislation."[52] And so this letter carries with it the clear implication of a threat: "Use what we approve or you don't get funded." Incidentally, the *Report of the National Reading Panel*, to which three of the letter's authors contributed, never recommended any reading series. Yet, here we have a letter essentially bullying the schools into using a program, or else no funding.

The point is that "scientifically approved" is a code for Open Court. Nationwide, this program has an enormous influence on what children learn and how they learn it. Therefore, we must look at its characteristics specifically, although they may also apply to other, less favored programs as well.

SCRIPTED MANUALS

Open Court is a tightly *scripted* program. This means that the teachers read directly from the manual as they move through the material. One of the defining elements of scripted programs such as Open Court is the pacing of lessons.

This pacing requires all teachers at a grade level to be on the same page at the same time on any given day. In fact, as part of its promotion, the publisher encourages districts to pay for coaches who are trained in the use of the program. The coaches sit in the classroom to make sure the teacher is following the manual and doesn't bring in books of her own or stray from the script.

This expensive training and the coaches' salaries are in addition to the high cost of the materials and profit the publishers.

Furthermore, the reasoning goes, teachers *want* to be told what to do.[53] So, because the materials are scripted and because coaches oversee the instruction based on the teacher manual, it is reasonable to conclude that *the reading series is in fact the reading curriculum*.

Now, as part of the requirements for receiving federal monies, in many states, funds for *professional development* must be spent on training teachers to use the required commercial reading series instead of on learning a variety of methods. As with the training and salaries of the Open Court coaches, the money goes to the publisher of the favored reading series. In times of budget cuts and deficits, with many states such as California and Oregon facing bankruptcy, many parents, teachers, and taxpayers object to these expensive programs and training at the same time that valid alternative programs are rejected by the federal grant overseers.

> The declared rationale behind the scripting of programs is that teachers are incapable of making decisions that affect the children in their own classrooms.

Questions for Discussion: If teachers must use a scripted, one-size-fits-all commercial program including highly regulated and restricted pacing, what is the role of the teacher? Who controls the schools, the classrooms, and the students? How does the mandating of tightly scripted programs fit into the law of local control? What does the use of programs such as Open Court mean for the future of teaching as a profession? What does it mean to be a teacher?

In spite of the problems with Open Court, we need to face the fact that there are some teachers who aren't very competent. New teachers are often confused and overwhelmed by the demands of facing a classroom for the first time. Therefore, don't basal reading series including Open Court help address these problems?

A basal reading series can provide some structure and some good ideas and can help teachers especially during the beginning year or so of teaching. However, we aren't talking about a tool and an opportunity for growth here. We're talking about a program and a national reading curriculum that are so tightly controlled that teachers are threatened with their jobs and are reprimanded by their principals if they stray from the program.

I've received dozens of letters from teachers across the country who recognize that Open Court is a flawed program that doesn't get good results but who are afraid to speak up. Here's a letter I received from a teacher. She gave me permission to use it if she could remain anonymous because she's afraid of negative repercussions for what she says about the Open Court program. That is quite a commentary on the level of intimidation that is associated with NCLB in general and with Open Court, specifically. I received this July 15, 2003:

Dear Elaine,

I just finished reading your book, *Resisting Reading Mandates*, and would like to thank you for writing it. I am just a lowly teacher. I say "lowly" because my influence is very small.

I am so concerned about the future of teaching reading that I am about ready to throw in the towel. I do believe in what I'm doing and in the children so I know that I have to keep trying, in my own small corner of the world, to do what I know in my heart and in my mind is right. I teach in—, in a school district that has mandated the use of Open Court.

I have to be very careful about what I say about Open Court *because it's almost heresy to suggest that something else might work as well or even better.* I don't know why these teachers won't say what they believe. *They are frustrated with it but they won't say anything against it. If they do, it's reported to the principal and he reprimands them for "being against OC."*

Even if I show them the information from your book, it won't change their minds. *Privately maybe, but not publicly.* I think that I need to do more than quietly go about my teaching but I am extremely non-confrontational and *I'm scared to take a stand that I know will be unpopular with my principal and some teachers.* I think that perhaps I need to go about quietly spreading a different opinion in a positive way that promotes good teaching practice but that, at the same time, does not vocally oppose OC. Do you have any suggestions for me?

Do you know what other teachers are doing out there who are in the same situation? I certainly feel as if I'm fighting a losing battle. I feel as if I'm not the only teacher in my district who opposes OC but since *everyone has to be so careful what they say, I don't know who else feels the same way I do. It's a despairing time for teachers right now. We can't give up but it just feels so hopeless.* (Emphasis mine.)

Sincerely—

How Do the Pros and Cons of Scripted Programs Affect Teachers and Students?

Point: The Case for Scripted Reading Programs

- Scripts mean that the curriculum is preset and standardized. Teachers do not need to prepare for classes or make decisions.
- All teachers at a grade level are on the same page at the same time. Therefore, it's easy to keep track of what they are doing.
- If schools are saturated with scripted—or even just tightly controlled—reading programs, teachers do not need to be educated in a variety of methods. The script will do their thinking for them.
- Businesses can run commercial teacher training programs set up as alternatives to traditional schools of education. Since the training is less comprehensive, it will be possible to pay the new-age teachers less money than more rigorously trained professionals.

As a California state legislator recently suggested to me, the current system imposed by the government with the help of its "reading experts" ensures a constant, regular turnover of teachers who are paid a miserly twenty-six thousand dollars, have no lasting commitment to the profession, and leave after two years of teaching. They never gain a foothold or become established or confident enough to pose a threat to the system that's in place.

Counterpoint: The Argument Against Scripted Programs

- Because all students are unique, a single method or standardized program doesn't work for all children.
- Teachers are intelligent. They can and they should be instructional leaders and make decisions in conjunction with other teachers and parents. They should be a part of the educational process instead of reading scripts and mouthing someone else's words and thoughts like ventriloquists' dummies.
- Because teaching is an art as well as a science, teachers need to understand children's growth and development.
- There is no research—government or otherwise—that supports the use of any commercial program.
- Scripted programs such as Open Court aren't new. They've been tried and ultimately rejected by schools for decades. It's a lot of money for a proven failure.

MORE INTIMIDATION

The level of intimidation extends beyond this particular teacher. On June 14, 2003, the *Fresno Bee* published a letter by a local teacher, Derek Boucher, criticizing the research base of Open Court Reading and questioning the financial links between the National Reading Panel contributors and McGraw-Hill Publishing. He used my book *Resisting Reading Mandates* as a source.[54] My book uses the data and the exact words of the government's own research, from the *Report of the National Reading Panel*, to refute McGraw-Hill's claims that Open Court Reading is a scientifically proven program. That NRP report and its alleged findings form the research base for President Bush's education mandates.

After the letter appeared, a national representative of McGraw-Hill contacted the paper. He denied that McGraw-Hill authors had any connection to the NRP and demanded a retraction from Mr. Boucher and from me too, although I had nothing to do with the letter. In fact, I knew nothing about it until days after it was published. I faxed the *Fresno Bee* the title page from the NRP report, listing Open Court authors Marilyn Adams and Michael Pressley as contributors, thus refuting McGraw-Hill's denial that its authors had any connection to the NRP. I also sent the documentation showing that Open Court author Marilyn Adams and another NRP contributor, Barbara Foorman, co-authored their own commercial phonemic awareness curriculum.

McGraw-Hill's Next Move

Faced with the black-and-white evidence of their Open Court authors' contributions to the NRP, McGraw-Hill moved to a new strategy of intimidation. In a follow-up exchange with Derek Boucher, a national representative of McGraw-Hill threatened to "publicize the fact that Elaine Garan was paid to write her book by a competitor of McGraw-Hill whose reading series was rejected." This statement is absolutely untrue. I have never worked for a publisher, never participated in any way, shape, or form in any reading series, much less served as a paid assassin for a competing reading series. McGraw-Hill is a big company with a lot of clout and a very extensive public relations machine.

A recurring theme throughout this discussion is scientific research. What are the research findings for Open Court? I hear that the program gets really good results.

What I'm telling you here about the research on Open Court is not a matter of interpretation. It is the data taken directly from the government's own NRP report. One of the studies in that scientific report looked at the effects of Open Court Reading on children in first and second grade (Table G, Study 11). In it we see two important findings:

First, the performance of the children who were trained with Open Court for an entire year dropped from first to second grade in *every skill that was tested. Every single one.*

Second, what's even more important is that in reading comprehension—the goal of reading—and in spelling, the scores dropped from +*0.19* (which is not even statistically significant to begin with) to –*0.19* by second grade.

What this huge drop in scores shows is that in this scientific research study, Open Court Reading, with its bottom-up, phonics-heavy approach to instruction, realizes the worst fears of so many teachers who oppose the program specifically and bottom-up, skills-focused instruction in general. Children focus on the skills and they do not apply them to authentic reading of *real* text. They think reading *is* the skills and the sounds instead of about making sense of text.

The NRP research for McGraw-Hill's program Direct Instruction, which is also sometimes known as DISTAR or Reading Mastery, shows a downward spiral that is similar to the drop that we see in Open Court. The children who were trained in Direct Instruction beginning in first grade and were taught using the program for three years showed a *negative* effect size (–0.12) for spelling. For comprehension, the results were not statistically different than zero (0.11). Again, we see that children didn't significantly benefit from expensive, long-term, bottom-up training in isolated skills and did not significantly transfer those skills to authentic text.[55]

Good teachers recognize that there is a difference between *learning to read* (in bottom-up instruction, this involves practice and regurgitation of separate skills) and *reading to learn* (the application of those skills to authentic textual readings). Therefore, if we accept the government's research as being sound, Open Court and Direct Instruction are failures if we want children to be good spellers and to understand what they read. Other programs showing negative findings in the NRP research are Orton-Gillingham and Jolly Phonics.[56] Therefore, we need to question the federal and state governments' mandating of such programs as well as any misrepresented findings touted by the program publishers.

Questions for Discussion: Are the ethics and business practices of publishers relevant to our decisions to use their products or to allow their involvement in the schools that serve our children? Should publishers be held accountable for misrepresenting government-sponsored research on their products? How does misrepresented research affect schools and children?

THE TRUTH ABOUT THE NRP FINDINGS ON COMMERCIAL READING PROGRAMS

I'm very confused. I've heard so much from publishers' representatives that their programs are scientifically proven. A lot of this discussion keeps coming back to the NRP report. Can you help me understand what this report, which is driving methods and materials, is all about?

What Is the NRP Report?

The National Reading Panel report was commissioned by Congress. The panel was appointed by the National Institute of Child Health and Human Development. The project director of NICHD was Louisa Moats, who, as we've seen, is also the research and professional development director of Sopris West, the company that publishes *Language!* The panel's purpose was to review the available research on reading instruction and to end the debate fueling the reading wars, once and for all. Finally, according to the propaganda, we would know the truth about the benefits of systematic, bottom-up phonics instruction. We can't afford to dismiss this report because it is its findings (supposedly) that drive the NCLB legislation. This report impacts every school, every teacher, every child, and every taxpayer in this country. It has a lot of clout.

The NRP Did Not Recommend Any Commercial Reading Program

In the phonics section, the NRP included the findings of a total of thirty-eight studies to draw its conclusions. Of those thirty-eight studies, twenty-eight involved commercial reading programs, including McGraw-Hill's programs Open Court and Direct Instruction (also called DISTAR or Reading Mastery). *Based on its research findings, the NRP did not recommend any commercial reading program—none.* If someone hands you a sales pitch and claims any different, ask her to show you where in the report such a recommendation is made. If she claims that her program has scientifically proven results based on the NRP phonics findings, ask her to show you the data from the report to support her claims. In fact, it would help if you ordered your own free copy of the report and highlighted the page numbers I provide here. You will have the evidence. She won't. I 100 percent guarantee it. You can order your very own copy of the NRP report for free at <*www.nationalreadingpanel.org*>. *Note:* There are at least three different versions of the report. They all look exactly the same and none is marked to indicate when the original report was revised, so your page numbers may differ somewhat. However, all the quotes that I provide here are in each version of the report.

As a matter of fact, not only did the NRP *not* recommend any commercial reading program, but it actually warned against the boring skill and drill of scripted programs and called for balanced reading.

Here's an exact quote: "*Some commercial programs are scripted in such a way that teacher judgment is largely eliminated. Although scripts may standardize instruction, they may reduce teachers' interest in the teaching process*" (2-96). The report states that scripted phonics programs may interfere not only with the learner's motivation to learn but with the teacher's motivation as well. The NRP report states, "It seems self-evident that teachers will be most effective when they are enthusiastic in their teaching and enjoy what they are doing in their classroom" (2-7). Period.

But while the NRP didn't recommend any one program, isn't it possible that its overall findings actually align with commercial programs and, therefore, those programs are scientifically sound?

You raise an interesting, important question here. How does systematic, bottom-up phonics instruction fare in the comprehensive NRP research?

A Quick Lesson on the NRP Research

I know that many teachers and parents are so busy with the day-to-day realities of teaching and parenting that they don't have the time and—in some cases—the background to come nose to nose with our government's research and critique it. But the Bush administration is counting on that. "Scientific research" is one of the thickest, most obtuse, most inscrutable curtains the reform Wizards have at their disposal. Whatever it claims, whatever programs it mandates, whatever sales pitch publishing giants sling at schools, the refrain is always the same: "Scientific research supports this. You must use this. If you don't, you're willfully depriving kids of the best methods and you don't deserve money just so you can continue bad medicine."

Therefore, we can't afford to ignore the research because it's in our schools and it's in our homes and it's hurting our kids. And we can't afford to be intimidated by it or we're at the mercy of the Bush administration and the publishing giants. Not only has the word *research* taken on a distinctly entrepreneurial cast, but it has now become a catchphrase for promoting a financial-political agenda. If we don't stand up to it, we surrender our power to the Enrons who are now controlling the schools.

What you need to know so you can talk back or at least think back to the lofty research infomercials is this: The NRP conducted what's called a *meta-analysis* on studies that looked at how phonics instruction impacts children's "reading." A meta-analysis is a statistical procedure that attempts to look across a number of studies on a particular topic and discover the overall results. In other words, one study on phonics might conclude that a given method works well, while another study could conclude that same method has failed. So a meta-analysis is a way to average out the findings of each individual study to draw some kind of reasonable, overall conclusion. Obviously, all the studies in a meta-analysis must measure the same outcome.

Of the thirty-eight studies the panel reviewed in its phonics section, all did experiments on children, so it's called *experimental research*—what is also referred to as a *medical model*. The NRP claims that the methodology it selected to review is the same kind of research used in medicine to promote "robust good health." In other words, our government claims to believe that methods used in physical or medical science are appropriate to use in studying human *behavior*.

Experimental research as used in the NRP-selected studies works like this: The researchers trained children in one group in a particular skill. Another group of children—called the *control group*—was *not* trained in the skill that the study was assessing. The skill being studied might include training the experimental children in a particular phonics sound and then testing their performance on identifying that sound in nonwords such as *dat, wat,* and *zat* from a list. Or the studies might test performance on a combination of skills such as reading a list of decodable words and identifying sight words on a list. All in all, there were six skills that any given study could look at:

1. Reading nonsense words from a list (regularly patterned nonwords such as *dat, wat, zat*)
2. Decoding (reading words from a list that all have a regular spelling pattern that can be sounded out, such as *cat, rat, hat*)
3. Word identification (reading words on lists that might be decodable and/or could include some sight words as well)
4. Spelling (For kindergarten and first grade, invented spelling was accepted as being correct. The only studies that insisted on conventional spelling as an outcome were those that applied to grades two through six.)
5. Oral reading (reading words in a text correctly; whether or not children comprehended was not a necessary element of the oral reading assessments)
6. Comprehension (In kindergarten and first grade, this involved mostly simple sentences with decodable text. For example, "Who sat on the rat?" Answer: "The cat." The tests in grades two through six used more complex passages to assess comprehension.)

While any study could look at from one to all six of these separate skills, none—not one study—looked at all six. Only 16 percent of the studies the panel used looked at comprehension. Nevertheless, the NRP somehow decided that the average of the separate skills for each study was called *reading growth*.

Questions for Discussion: Since most of the studies did not assess comprehension, consider the panel's use of the term *reading growth*. What does the selection of this term say about the panel's view of the reading process? Most of the panel members were bottom-up, skills researchers. They were not classroom teachers. How might their experimental skills-based research background color their approach to the research and taint their conclusions? How might their lack of experience in actually teaching children to read affect their understanding of how *real* children react in *real* classroom situations? What is the role of comprehension in reading? Is there true reading growth without comprehension?

Answer: National Reading Panel Leaves Children's Comprehension Behind

As we saw, in the NRP's assortment of studies, the children were tested at the end of the experiments to see which group—the trained, experimental group or the untrained control group—performed better on the skill that the experimental group was trained in. The results for all thirty-eight studies were put on a chart that showed the individual and assorted skills that each study assessed. For each study, a separate column showed the average *effect size*—think result(s)—for each study. Then the averages of the thirty-eight studies were averaged yet again. This final averaging was the end goal of the phonics meta-analysis.

Now, here's what we need to really pay attention to: As we saw, the panel called this final average of all the phonics studies **reading growth.** Nearly three-quarters (74 percent) of the studies looked at *only* bottom-up skills without considering comprehension. So we can draw two conclusions here.

First, the term **reading growth,** assigned by the panel to describe its findings, is a misnomer because the majority of the studies did not look at reading growth at all, but only at pieces of skills such as sounding out nonwords or identifying words on lists, which, as any teacher knows, is very different than actually reading a book. Another way to put it is that only 24 percent of the studies even required the children to read from a book and 8 percent of that number involved oral reading, which is *not* a test of comprehension. So, only 16 percent of those results that the panel somehow decided determined reading growth even looked at comprehension. Most teachers and parents agree that comprehension is the ultimate goal of reading.

Second, since the majority of the studies looked at only one or a very few isolated skills, it's fair to say that not only is the phonics section of the NRP report a good indicator of what happens when children are trained in isolated skills, but the phonics section is a window into the effects of bottom-up instruction. In truth, most of the NRP studies never even got beyond "bottom." They never moved to the "up" of real reading and comprehension. With that caution in mind, let's look at how the teaching of isolated phonics skills affected children's ability to really read and spell according to the NRP's own "highly scientific" research study. In other words, let's meet them on their own scientific ground. Let's play their own game using their own rules and see how isolated phonics instruction did.

The Bottom Line on the Effects of Bottom-Up Teaching on Comprehension

According to the NRP's findings, bottom-up phonics instruction did not significantly benefit children's comprehension of real or "connected text" or their conventional spelling *at any grade level.* This is not my interpretation. This is based on the NRP's own findings. The comprehension for kindergarten and first graders involved short, decodable passages ("The fat cat sat")—not real, connected text.

For older students, bottom-up phonics instruction never moved significantly off the bottom rung. Phonics did not significantly benefit comprehension. Here are the panel's *own findings* in its *own words,* directly from the NRP report: "The comprehension of text *was not significantly improved*" by systematic phonics instruction (*Summary Booklet,* 9). "Systematic phonics instruction *failed to exert a significant impact* on the reading performance [of the students the studies assessed] in 2nd through 6th grade" (NRP report, 2-88). The NRP report continues, "phonics instruction appears to *contribute only weakly, if at all* in helping [the students the studies assessed] apply these [decoding skills] to read text and to spell words" (2-108). Again, this is not my interpretation. It is the National Reading Panel's conclusions.

The Bottom Line on the Effects of Bottom-Up Teaching on Spelling

Systematic phonics instruction did not significantly benefit children's conventional spelling at any grade level, either. For kindergarten and first grade, the studies in the NRP report accepted invented spellings as being correct (*ft* for *foot*). Here, in the panel's *own words,* are the findings for the impact of phonics on spelling from second through sixth grade: "The effect size for spelling [for children in 2nd through 6th grade] *was not statistically different from zero* (.09) . . . [phonics was] *not more effective than other forms of instruction* in producing growth in spelling" (2-108).

Here's one more important research fact: A team of researchers led by Gregory Camilli did an independent reanalysis of the NRP report on phonics. They examined the panel's procedures and conducted their own meta-analysis using the same studies. Camilli's group found that

1. The NRP used an incorrect statistical measure that overestimated the effects of phonics.
2. The NRP paid a lot of attention to the selection procedures for picking the studies but too little time actually analyzing them: "Perhaps [the] inattention to analytical issues is because . . . the NRP interpreted 'rigorous standards' to mean 'rigorous selection criteria' for including studies, but the results of a meta-analysis depend as much on the rigor of the analytic procedures." In fact, the NRP included one incorrect formula.
3. When the Camilli group correctly reanalyzed the data, the NRP studies showed that when language activities were combined with phonics, the effect size tripled that of phonics alone.
4. The NRP defined *reading* as performance on isolated skills, *not* as the reading of text with comprehension as a necessary outcome.

And so, the Camilli team concluded, "As federal policies are formulated around early literacy curricula and instruction, these findings indicate that phonics, as one aspect of the complex reading process, should not be over-emphasized."[57] Camilli and his team are not reading experts and they say this right up front. They have no stake in the reading wars. They looked at the data.

Somehow, panel member Timothy Shanahan managed to interpret Camilli's study as support for the NRP findings and ignored the caveats, the errors, and the biases Camilli's team documents.[58] These include that the NRP overstated and misrepresented its findings. Shanahan states, "I am very pleased that in spite of making important changes in the analysis itself, the authors came to the same general conclusion that we did (albeit with a lower effect size). Phonics instruction clearly gives kids a benefit." Shanahan also claims that criticisms of the NRP report are based on procedural rather than on substantive errors.[59] This assertion is puzzling to say the least, because the methodology obviously affects the outcome of any research and this panel staked a claim to using rigorous scientific procedures.

Let's think about Shanahan's response to criticism of the NRP. His reaction is at once an admission and a denial. It seems the NRP shot the sheriff, but it did not shoot the deputy, so we should all be grateful to it. It's as if the panel were saying, "Well, now that your mechanic has caught us in the act of misrepresenting the quality of this used car, well, sure—the engine and the transmission don't work. But the windshield wipers are in pretty good shape. You have my word on it. So buy it anyway." Does that make any sense to you?

As we will see, the flaws in the report affect not just the procedures but the very heart of the NRP's research, including the ongoing, very basic misrepresentation of the report's findings.

Questions for Discussion: How do the reading methods and the commercial reading series used in your school or your child's class reflect the true findings of the NRP report? How do the bottom-up methods and materials the federal government is mandating reflect the *true* findings of its own NRP's research? Why would our government mandate methods and commercial reading programs that don't significantly benefit comprehension and spelling?

I'm very confused. Not only have I heard the opposite about the research results for Open Court, but I've seen newspaper headlines claiming that the NRP found that phonics benefited children at all grade levels. Our district recently applied for a Reading First grant and we were told we must use a scientifically proven core program such as Open Court. What's going on?

What you need to understand is this: The NRP report comes in three different formats, each of them bound separately.

The *first* is the *Report of the Subgroups,* which is more than five hundred pages in length. It contains all the actual data and information and discussion on the studies and the findings.

The *second* format is a 15-minute video that ostensibly summarizes the findings. It includes clips of teachers and children using Open Court as well as comments by a couple of panel members.

The *third* format is a short summary booklet that's thirty-two pages in length. *It is this summary booklet that forms the basis of current legislation and mandates. It has been distributed to thousands of teachers and administrators.*

Here's the problem: The conclusions in the NRP summary do *not* match the data in the actual report!

So, the report itself says phonics does *not* significantly affect comprehension and spelling. It also says that the findings apply *only* to children with reading problems for kindergarten, second, third, fourth, fifth, and sixth grades—*not normally progressing readers, not children for whom English is a second language, not low-achieving readers, not gifted children.*[60] In fact, the findings, dismal as they are, do not apply to the majority of the school population.

And yet, the neat little summary booklet states, "The meta-analysis revealed that systematic phonics instruction produces significant benefits for students in kindergarten through sixth grade *and* for children having difficulty learning to read" (emphasis mine). *Now,* here again is the quote from the big, thick report of the subgroups: "*Phonics instruction appears to contribute only weakly, if at all in helping [the students the studies assessed] apply these [decoding skills] to read text and to spell words*" (2-108).

That's incredible! I can't believe my eyes. I checked my copy of the NRP report. It was very frustrating because the page numbers were different than what you listed here, just as you say, so it was really hard to find those quotes, but you're right. I'm outraged that our tax dollars are going to programs based on false conclusions!

Wait! There's more. The NRP *Summary Booklet* states: "Across *all* grade levels systematic phonics instruction improved the ability of good readers to spell" (10, emphasis mine).

Now, you might want to move your cat off your lap. Here are the actual findings in the report: "*The effect size for spelling [for children in 2nd through 6th grade] was not statistically different from zero (.09) . . . [phonics was] not more effective than other forms of instruction in producing growth in spelling"* (2-108).

Surely by now the scientific National Reading Panel has recognized its errors and corrected them so that schools aren't being forced to use programs and methods based on false research, right?

There were fourteen members on the NRP, as well as panel contributors. To date, five panel members or contributors have admitted that the summary (on which our legislation is based) doesn't match the findings.[61] For example, panel contributor Barbara Foorman states, "The National Reading Panel Summary is intended for a general audience and anyone who reads only the Summary is likely to be misinformed."[62]

Now, three years after its release and after five panel members or contributors have admitted that the summary doesn't match the findings, let us go to the website of the National Reading Panel. What follows here was cut and pasted directly from that website, *<www.nationalreadingpanel.org>*, on August 2, 2003:

Publications and Materials
NRP Publications and Materials

Report of the National Reading Panel
"Teaching Children to Read" | Summary Report

The Summary Report is **an ideal resource for anyone** who wants to understand the purpose, methodology, and results of the National Reading Panel's findings on reading instruction research.

This 32-page report explains the origin of the Panel and its congressional charge. It succinctly describes the research methodology used and the findings of each of the Panel subgroups: (1) Alphabetics, (2) Fluency, (3) Comprehension, (4) Teacher Education and Reading Instruction, and (5) Computer Technology and Reading Instruction. *This report also offers insightful information provided by Panel members on reading instruction* topics that may require further exploration.

This report is an excellent resource for parents, teachers, administrators, or anyone interested in learning about reading instruction research. (Emphasis mine.)

I checked the NRP website and again, you're right! But I thought the NRP report is supposed to represent the highest, most scientific standards for rigorous, objective research. How could such a startling discrepancy continue to exist? It seems that the errors in the reporting are not incidental but are central to the accuracy of the research. How could such misrepresented information continue to control the materials and methods used in schools?

I don't know. No one on the panel has ever answered that question. Nor has our secretary of education, nor has President Bush or his top reading advisor, Reid Lyon. So all we can do is look at the facts: The NRP summary (inaccurately reporting the findings) was written in part by *Widmeyer-Baker*, the public relations firm that Open Court's publisher, *McGraw-Hill*, pays to promote its products. Here's something else to think about: The video of the National Reading Panel shows clips of children being drilled in McGraw-Hill's Open Court even though the report itself does not recommend any commercial program and warns against the use of scripted programs. The video is available for free at the NRP website. Oh, and those "free" videos and NRP documents are paid for by our tax dollars.

As a matter of fact, go to the NRP website, <*www .nationalreadingpanel.org*>, and click on "Press Releases and Testimony" and then on "Press Releases." You can then peruse the minutes of NRP proceedings documenting that McGraw-Hill's public relations firm played an active role in determining the slant of the findings. Furthermore, that firm directed the video our taxes are subsidizing. This amounts to more than just publicizing findings. It means that the promoter of a commercial reading series played a crucial role in the directing and ultimately the shaping not just of public opinion, which is dangerous enough, but of education legislation.[63]

It doesn't seem right that McGraw-Hill's PR agency should have a role that's so influential that it could misrepresent the findings, thereby determining education policy. Why haven't

*the panel members objected or gone before Congress or called
a press conference and demanded that their findings be
represented accurately? I'm shocked that they haven't!*

The only panel member to take a proactive role in speaking out
against the misrepresentations is Joanne Yatvin, who wrote a minority report as well as articles documenting the flawed and sub-
jective procedures of the NRP.[64]

Other panel members responded when they were cornered.
But their admissions were published in scholarly journals. To my
knowledge, they did not use their role as NRP members to address Congress or to hold press conferences to make any viable, strenuous objections to the continuing misrepresentations of
their work. Most of the panel members have made no comment
at all.

*But why haven't they spoken out? Surely they ought to be
calling press conferences and addressing Congress about the
misuse of their work. I know I would. Why haven't they?*

The Objectivity of the NRP Scientists

It's hard to ascribe motives to anyone's actions. But again, we can
look at the facts and then you can draw your own conclusions.
Obviously, one of the basic tenets of any ethical research is that
not only is it open to scrutiny, but it welcomes such scrutiny.
How, then, have the scientifically committed panelists reacted to
the critiques documenting their errors—not just in procedures
but in the reporting and, therefore, the use of the NRP results?

Answer: While the other, more cooperative panel members
have their expenses paid by NICHD for speaking engagements,
NRP panel member Dr. Joanne Yatvin pays her own. And in a
symposium on the National Reading Panel held in Los Angeles
in 2001, when panel member Sally Shaywitz introduced the
panel members by pointing to their pictures on an easel, she
skipped over and totally omitted any mention of Joanne Yatvin
as a panel member. Such is the dedication to scientific scrutiny,
objectivity, and accuracy that we see in the public posture of
panel members.[65] At best, this was tacky and small-minded. At
worst, it is a way of rewriting history, to say nothing of the NRP's
claim to a concerted, objective research effort.

In all fairness, the National Institute of Child Health and Human Development, which sponsored the NRP, picked that panel well. As we've seen, with the exception of Yatvin, for the most part, the rest of the panel members have stood by silently, or made tepid admissions, but have generally circled the wagons and allowed public policy to be framed on research that they know full well is verifiably inaccurate. And not a peep from any of them about Widmeyer-Baker's role in the proceedings, either.

Why would the panelists continue to support false findings?

As I said, it's hard to ascribe personal and professional motives to anyone's actions. For that reason in legal proceedings, judges and lawyers are ethically bound to remove or recuse themselves from participation in matters in which they have a vested personal or financial interest so there isn't even the *appearance* of impropriety. Unfortunately, we see many links between the scientific researchers, the falsely reported findings, and their lucrative involvement in their own commercial reading program enterprises—and the administration of President Bush.

But I read a statement by Barbara Foorman, who is an NRP contributor. In a letter to Phi Delta Kappan, she asks, "Where is the evidence for the implied conflict of interest [involving the NRP]?"[66]

Well, here it is. In my last book, *Resisting Reading Mandates*, I said that I'd tried to make a flowchart showing the conflicts of interest among panel members, the products they're selling, the research, and the Bush administration, but that it was like trying to unravel a plate of worms. The only difference now, two years later, is that there are more worms on the plate.

The links among researchers, politics, and big money are so incestuous that a flowchart is impossible. I'll **boldface** the major players and the money-political links so it's a little easier for you to follow. Of course, keep this in mind: The fact that these scientists stand to make money on their research may be entirely incidental to the misreported, misapplied findings. Likewise, the fact that Chester Finn has a vested interest in his own for-profit alternative to public schools may not color his judgment in making recommendations for public school "reform." Here we go.

Barbara Foorman

Barbara Foorman denies that she reviewed her own studies in her role as contributor to the NRP report. In a letter to *Phi Delta Kappan*, she claims she was "only" a "technical advisor" to the phonics and phonemic awareness sections.[67] However, during the NRP research proceedings, the panel had a mailing list server. Panel member Joanne Yatvin saved those communications, which show that Foorman was indeed a reviewer of the alphabetics section.

Foorman also has her own commercial phonemic awareness program that she coauthored with another NRP contributor, **Marilyn Adams,** who just happens to be an author of McGraw-Hill's Open Court Reading and is also the author of another government-sponsored report, *Beginning to Read*.[68] Therefore, Adams has a lot of research clout. As a matter of fact, the Open Court series boasts that Adams is "cited in the 2000 Politics of Education Yearbook as one of the *five most influential people in the national reading policy arena*" (emphasis mine.) And so we have an indisputable link between yet another major public policy-maker and her own for-profit use of research paid for with our tax dollars. Of course, this doesn't mean that their financial interests motivated Adams and Foorman in their research or in their influence in framing public policy.

The coauthors of Foorman and Adams' profitable commercial program are **Ingvar Lundberg** and **Terri Beeler.** Three of their studies are included in the phonemic awareness section of the NRP report, one of the sections for which their coauthor, Foorman, was the "technical advisor." Four of the thirty-eight studies in the phonics section are by Barbara Foorman.[69]

Conclusion 1: Both Foorman and Adams have a commercial interest in the promotion of phonics and phonemic awareness as well as influence over public education policy.

Conclusion 2: Foorman was a "technical advisor" and reviewer of not only her own studies but those conducted by the coauthors of her commercial phonemic awareness curriculum.

Conclusion 3: The misreported findings in the summary make false claims for the impact of phonics and apply them to all children in kindergarten through grade six.

You can buy the phonemic awareness program profiting these NRP panel contributors through Amazon. Just look for *Phonemic Awareness in Young Children: A Classroom Curriculum*.[70] You can buy Open Court Reading from McGraw-Hill Publishing. You can get the NRP report, which your tax dollars subsidized, for "free."

Louisa Moats

There's more. Louisa Moats is the project director of NICHD, our government agency that sponsored the NRP report. Moats is also the research and professional development director for her own entrepreneurial pursuit, a commercial program called *Language!* that pushes decodable "Cat spat at rat" programs on middle and high school students. The companies that distribute *Language!* are **Sopris West** and . . . **McGraw-Hill/Glencoe.**[71] Thus, the program Moats is selling carries with it the cachet and the clout of her role as NICHD director.

In fact, the professional training for teachers—you remember, the training Moats directs at Sopris West—begins with a clip from the NRP video that was directed by **Widmeyer-Baker,** McGraw-Hill's PR agency.[72]

Recall that our tax dollars paid for this video. During *Language!* professional development training, the NRP segment shown states, "Now we know through science how kids learn to read," the *Language!* presentation then extols the use of phonics and decodable text such as that used in *Language!* This in spite of the fact that the NRP did not even include research on kids above sixth grade *or* on decodable text *and* in spite of the fact that above first grade, phonics did not help kids' reading growth, as we've seen!

Wait. There's still more on *Language!* The only "research" for this program—besides the implied blessing of the NRP findings—was done by **Jane Fell Greene** . . . the creator of *Language!*[73] On its website, you will see that *Language!* is not only "research based" but is "Commended for Excellence" and has been "Adopted by the State of California" from 1999 through 2005. And so this program is approved for middle and high school students, based on one study—done by its creator—published in a journal on dyslexia. It doesn't take a rocket scientist to see serious problems with this whole scenario.

Incidentally, if you want to reach Louisa Moats, you can email her at Sopris West at *louisam@sopriswest.com*. I don't know how you can reach her at NICHD, where our tax dollars are paying for her research expertise. Perhaps someone at Sopris West or McGraw-Hill/Glencoe could give you her NICHD address.

Linnea Ehri

Ehri was the chair of the Alphabetics Committee of the NRP. She was also a paid research consultant to **Houghton Mifflin's** reading series and her name is included in that series as a "consultant." Ehri's contributions preceded the NRP report, and in all fairness, she may have been paid one set fee with no ongoing royalties.

However, Houghton Mifflin uses Ehri's role as its consultant *and* her connection to the NRP in its sales presentations. In California, state law requires that schools have a choice of five reading series. In spite of this law, we had only two choices. One was Houghton Mifflin and the other was McGraw-Hill's Open Court. Both of these series could boast authors and/or consultants who participated in the NRP report.

The press release heralding the completion of the NRP report by the chair of the NRP, **Donald Langenberg,** clearly states that the panel *reviewed* studies in order to draw its conclusions.[74] In her role as chair of the Alphabetics Committee, Ehri, like Foorman, was in a position to review her own studies because her work is among the research on which the NRP findings are based. One of the tenets of peer-reviewed research is that it is blind. That is, the authors' names are removed from studies before review in order to diffuse any possible prejudicial treatment in the reviews. It is reasonable to assume that Ehri and Foorman recognized their own work and, therefore, by the scholarly standards of the profession, the NRP's report can hardly be called an independent, peer-reviewed scholarly effort.

McGraw-Hill Publishing

Recall the Adams–Foorman–NICHD research–Open Court connection? Now let's examine the links between the publisher of the Open Court and Direct Instruction commercial programs, the NICHD researcher-contributors, and the White House. After the inauguration of George W. Bush, one of the first visitors to the White House was none other than **Harold McGraw III,** chairman and chief executive of the nation's largest K–12 publisher. Such a visit was not surprising, since McGraw was on the board of directors of the **Barbara Bush Foundation.**[75] And so we see a publishing mogul with input into education policy that has continued over a number of years. In 1990, Harold McGraw Junior's "support of literacy," which just may have profited his own company, earned him the nation's highest literacy award, presented by President George Bush in 1990.

Harold McGraw Jr. gave a million dollars to the Hechinger Institute for Education and the Media at Columbia University to sponsor an annual seminar (free) for new education reporters. Such "educational" initiatives may explain the pro-phonics, back-to-basics slant that permeates the media and "informs" the public. Now, as a reminder, lest you lose track of all the McGraw-Hill–Bush–public policy connections, there is NRP contributor and Open Court author Marilyn Adams, who as we have seen is linked to NRP research and to public education policy, and her phonemic awareness curriculum coauthor Barbara Foorman, who was a "technical advisor" to the NRP. Are you starting to see a clear pattern of government-policy-money links? More . . .

George W. Bush selected Marilyn Adams and four other McGraw-Hill authors to guide his Texas reading initiative. Now let's continue the Texas–McGraw–resesearch–science–Bush administration links. Secretary of Education Rod Paige also has links to McGraw-Hill Publishing.

Rod Paige, Secretary of Education
We recall that G. W. Bush is the former governor of Texas and that Harold McGraw Jr. was a member of the board of directors of the Barbara Bush Foundation and that four McGraw-Hill authors were consultants for the Texas initiative. Rod Paige was superintendent for the Houston Independent School District until 2001. As such, he solicited input from business leaders for strengthening school support services and programs.

Paige launched a system of charter schools and had broad authority in decisions regarding staffing, textbooks, and materials as well as increased testing. Shortly after the Houston schools implemented McGraw-Hill's Open Court program, Paige was awarded the Harold W. McGraw Jr. Educator of the Year Award for his "service."[76] This award included a large cash bonus. Rod Paige is now a strong proponent for the "scientific research"

sponsored by NICHD, which as we have seen is replete with entrepreneurial researchers such as Open Court author Marilyn
Adams and one of the coauthors of her commercial phonemic
awareness program, Barbara Foorman.

As we've seen, Paige claims, "There is not an 'approved list' of
programs and materials to be used in connection with Reading
First." He says this in spite of his selection of Open Court for the
Houston schools. Nevertheless, both he *and* George W. Bush
have made what sounds very much like public endorsements of
the **Voyager Learning** program. In fact, you can find these on the
Voyager website. They're part of the company's sales brochure.
Here's what they said:

> *Rod Paige:* In the Houston Independent School District, we
> are determined to teach all our children to read, and we expect
> the Voyager Universal Literacy System to be a major factor in
> our quest for 100% literacy.

> *Governor George W. Bush (who is now President Bush):* The
> Voyager Expanded Learning program is making a big differ-
> ence in people's lives. The philosophy behind this program is
> one that says we're going to teach every child to soar.[77]

Can you see how school districts could be led to believe that
there *are* approved programs and that McGraw-Hill and Voyager
are the publishers of those core reading and supplemental programs? We have actions telling us certain programs and publishers are approved. And we have the words of our president and
our secretary of education.

Incidentally, in what I suppose some might describe as a testa-
ment to the efficiency of scientific rigor, the same Voyager brochure that touts the endorsements by Rod Paige and George W.
Bush also informs us how anyone can get a Reading Specialist
certificate in just four days. Perhaps just coincidentally, of
course, Voyager's founder, **Randy Best,** and Voyager investors
made "generous contributions" to the campaign of then-Gover-
nor George W. Bush, according to the *Dallas Morning News*. Oh,
and Bush's former Texas Education Commissioner, **Jim Nelson,**
took a job at Voyager. But the fact that Voyager made campaign
contributions to Governor Bush *just* when the company was bid-

ding to run after-school programs in Texas may have no connection at all to Bush's endorsement of Voyager. Or Rod Paige's either. It might all be just more of the coincidences that characterize the relationship between the money, the researchers, the politicians, and the programs that are declared to be "scientific."[78]

But there's more. Do you remember who conducted the "scientific research" on Voyager? It's **Joseph Torgesen,** one of Voyager's own design team members, who also just happens to be a big player and governmental research grant recipient in Florida, the state governed by **Jeb Bush,** George W. Bush's brother. Does Joe Torgesen's research focus here remind you at all of Jane Fell Greene's "scientific research" on her own program, *Language!*, whose research director is also the project director of NICHD— you remember, "scientific" researcher Louisa Moats? And remember that her program is distributed by McGraw-Hill.

Here are more connections. Other Voyager design team members are McGraw-Hill authors **Edward J. Kame'enui** and **Deborah C. Simmons,** who also wrote **Reading Language Arts Framework for California.**[79] They constructed the rubric that schools must use to comply with scientific standards, although the language arts framework *preceded* the NRP report! Guess whose bottom-up sequence and methodology the framework of these McGraw-Hill authors matches? Might this link explain why California schools could choose from only two approved programs instead of the five the law promises us?

Another Bush family member, **Neil Bush,** has his own educational software enterprise, called **Ignite.**

Too Many Colors

For one of my presentations, I made an overhead transparency of some of the vested financial interests of the "scientific researchers" and their connections to government policy. I tried color coding to make the links easier to follow. When I came to Edward Kame'enui, I ran out of colors. He has financial links at so many levels, I can't list them all here. He and **Douglas Carnine,** another researcher-mogul out of the University of Oregon, are both McGraw-Hill authors. Kame'enui also has interests in the testing and is one of the creators of **DIBELS,** an "approved" test for oral reading fluency. On the DIBELS homepage, you see that most of the research support for DIBELS was done by members of the Voyager design team, including Torgesen (again), **Roland Good III,** and of course, Kame'nui.[80] Oh, and DIBELS is distributed by Sopris West/McGraw-Hill.

Incidentally, Kame'enui and Simmons also serve as advisors for **Reading First grants** and helped write the "scientific" criteria for grant acceptance, including the core programs to be used, the supplemental programs, the teacher training, and the assessments. So we have Kame'enui reaping the rewards of his "research" at every level of our government's "reform." It's like the house that Jack built: They

> do the research
> that supports their programs
> that match the assessments they designed
> that support their own programs
> that align with government mandates
> that are based on their scientific research.

And so on and so on and so on and so on. I'm getting a headache from trying to link it all and so I'm going to stop because this could go on for several more pages, but I think you get the point.

One suggestion: When you see a name or a program touted as being "scientific," do a quick Google search on the program's authors and the "researchers." If you begin a pattern of looking closely, you'll begin to notice that many of the educational summits organized by our department of education public servants are run by "business leaders" as part of "business roundtables." You'll also notice that government leaders such as Rod Paige do a lot of speaking at meetings sponsored by corporations. Don't be fooled by titles such as "Dr." or "researcher," either. In many cases, as we've seen, behind that curtain lurk entrepreneurs with their own products to sell.

Of course, this all may be for the public good rather than the good of the corporations. But it's something to think about, isn't it?

I can see why you have a headache, but I hope you'll answer a question for me. Many of the names I see here, such as Kame'enui, Torgesen, Simmons, and Carnine, are people who are associated with special education. How can their research—as entrepreneurially energetic as it is—apply to normal populations? Do these guys think all children have learning problems? Is this acceptable in research? I noticed that the NRP phonics studies focused on special education populations, too.

I'm going to refer back to the analogy you suggested in Section 2 and expand on it. Just maybe, when the foxes have the power to give better-living seminars for chickens, they stop seeing chickens. They start to see dinner. On the other hand, maybe these links between the researchers, the financial interests, and the government are all really totally irrelevant.

Most of the studies in the NRP were conducted by "researchers" in special education on children with learning problems. It is a basic tenet of any ethical research that the findings must be restricted to the population on which the studies were conducted. Furthermore, as we saw, the findings were dismal and were misreported, to say nothing of the stranglehold this lopsided "science" has inflicted on our children, our teachers, and our schools. Most of the NRP studies looked at commercial programs and were conducted by designers or authors or stakeholders in those programs. Programs such as McGraw-Hill's Open Court and Direct Instruction were designed for special education students and have a history of failure. As Reading Hall of Fame member and researcher Dr. Richard Allington notes:

> Given that direct-instruction programs for children identified as learning disabled have been just about the most disastrously unsuccessful educational efforts offered in American schools, it seems almost lunacy that so many of the entrepreneurs of that approach are now offering advice on improving classroom instruction. . . .

> It would have made sense to me if the politicians had stepped in and eliminated the NICHD and the Office of Special Education and Rehabilitation Services because of their almost complete failure to educate the learning disabled children entrusted to them. But putting the special education direct-instruction gurus in charge of reforming American reading instruction—even Orwell wouldn't have imagined such an outcome.[81]

I want to suggest questions for discussion here, but it's hard to come up with one that isn't so obvious that it won't provoke authentic debate. Here's the best I can do.

Questions for Discussion: Can the financial interests of researchers who shape educational policy color their findings, even inadvertently? Should such conflicts of interest be allowed to exist, much less to shape the direction of education in the country? Why has this takeover by entrepreneurial research been allowed to thrive under the name of science?

Before we move on to top-down instruction, I want to close here with the words of Albert Einstein, who was by anyone's standards a scientist. He was also keenly aware of the dangers of imposing scientific methods on human problems. He also understood the moral imperatives that must attend scientific principles.

> WHAT NEED IS THERE FOR A CRITERION OF RESPONSIBILITY? I believe that the horrifying deterioration in the ethical conduct of people today stems primarily from the mechanized dehumanization of our lives—a disastrous byproduct of the development of the scientific and technical mentality. . . . Man grows cold faster than the planet he inhabits.
>
> Albert Einstein, letter to Dr. Otto Juliusburger,
> April 11, 1946

So, now that we've looked at the bottom-up philosophy of reading and the materials, methods, and research that drive this view of learning, we'll compare it with a top-down view of reading.

Section VII

TOP-DOWN TEACHING, METHODS, MATERIALS, AND RESEARCH

READING INSTRUCTION: A QUICK OVERVIEW OF A TOP-DOWN CLASSROOM

As we've seen, bottom-up classrooms evoke the familiar image of the teacher at the front of the class, teacher-generated questions, and seatbound, relatively passive students. The curriculum is virtually controlled by the basal reading series and so is the teacher, particularly if the program is scripted and pacing is maintained by coaches.

More Student Talk

Top-down classrooms look, sound, and feel very different than what most of us have experienced. In top-down classes, students are usually seated in groups and do lots of planning and working on projects with each other. Students talk more in top-down classes, not just to the teacher but to each other, too. It's fair to say that top-down classes can be noisier than traditional bottom-up classrooms, where student talk is actually discouraged.

More Reading and Writing

Students do a lot of reading in top-down classes. And the term *reading* is defined differently than in bottom-up classes, where *reading* means worksheets and skills practice. In top-down classes, students practice reading by using real books that they've selected themselves.

Even writing looks different than in bottom-up classes. The teacher's goal is to establish a classroom community that resembles real life as much as possible. So skills aren't pulled out of their context and drilled on worksheets. As much as possible, they are learned as they are used and as they are needed.

I'm not sure I like the idea of students talking to each other and working together. They don't have the social skills or the maturity to do that without a lot of arguing. The whole idea sounds very chaotic to me.

A top-down teacher would say that in some ways you're right. Kids do lack the skills to work together. But she would say that is exactly the point. How can they learn these skills and how can they assume the responsibility for their social as well as their academic behavior—the kinds of skills they'll need in real-life work and in real-life relationships—if we don't teach them (not preach, but teach them) how to work together in school? In real life, there is no teacher looking over our shoulders, directing and controlling our every action.

But look, right now, this is all very abstract for you. Let's come back to the point about social skills and the way the methods and materials teachers use affect more than kids' academic performance. We'll see whether they *socialize* children into being either independent thinkers and doers or relatively mindless followers after we've examined top-down methods concretely. I think it will all make more sense to you later than it does right now. Let's start with writing instruction, because in top-down classrooms it looks very different than it does in traditional, skills-based, bottom-up teaching. In fact, writing is so closely connected to reading that there is no distinct boundary between them.

Writing in Top-Down Classrooms

Unlike bottom-up teachers, top-down teachers believe that children need to start writing even before they can read and **as** they are learning to read. As soon as children come to school, they begin writing their own messages and stories. Writing in top-down classrooms looks very different than the copying and filling in the blanks and formulaic kinds of rote writing that tend to characterize bottom-up classes.

How can kindergarten children write when they don't even know their letters and sounds and when they can't read yet?

You'd be surprised at how much young children know about the way print works before they even come to school! Many very young children have some sense that writing is made up of letters and that it is supposed to carry a message. Some know that print goes from left to right. And you're correct in your assumption that young children still don't necessarily spell correctly, but top-down teachers believe that when we encourage them to write using temporary or invented spelling, they don't lose sight of the fact that print is about making meaning, not about copying words or paragraphs from the board that they can't even read yet, but about expressing their ideas and feelings, too.

That sounds all warm and fuzzy, but the whole idea of "express yourself" and forget about spelling and grammar is at the root of the decline of good writing and high standards. I've seen lots of articles about the dangers of invented spelling, including one in People *magazine that quotes Louisa Moats. Why would any teacher in her right mind encourage sloppy, incorrect writing and spelling? No wonder we're turning into a society of functionally illiterate dropouts!*

You've expressed a huge misconception about invented spelling. Moats and others who have programs to sell would have us all believe that the only way to write is to make sure every word is spelled correctly from the beginning. First, this gives kids the idea that the purpose of writing is spelling and letter formation— instead of the idea that spelling is a tool to make our message clear to the reader.

Second, if children's writing comes back all marked up, and, as some bottom-up teachers demand, children are forced to correct misspelled words and practice writing those words five or ten times, how do you think children will react?

Let me give you an example here of the writing of two second-grade children. I gathered them when I was doing writing workshops in New Mexico. These children were the same age and in the same school and the samples were taken within the same week. They were in different classes—one with a bottom-up and one with a top-down teacher, respectively (see Figure 3).

Questions for Discussion: Look at the samples in Figure 3 and discuss what they tell us about what each of these children knows

FIGURE 3 Writing Samples

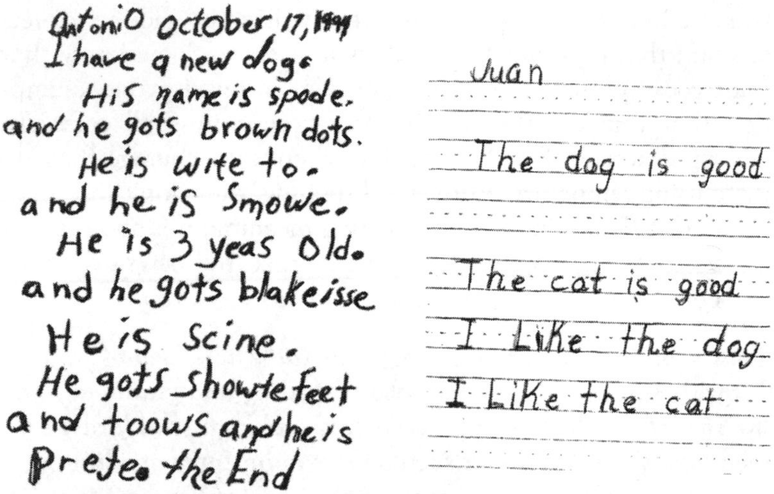

Antonio october 17, 1991
I have a new dogs
   His name is spode.
and he gots brown dots.
   He is wite to.
and he is Smowe.
   He is 3 yeas Old.
and he gots blakeisse
   He is Scine.
   He gots Showte feet
and toows and he is
Prete. the End

Juan

The dog is good

The cat is good
I Like the dog
I Like the cat

"Translation" of Antonio's story:
I have a new dog.
   His name is Spotty.
And he gots brown dots.
   He is white too.
And he is small.
   He is 3 years old.
And he gots black eyes.
   He is skinny.
   He gots short feet
and toes. And he is
pretty.
The End

about writing. What does Juan think the purpose of writing is? Why did he choose the words he did? Do you see a resemblance between his writing and the controlled vocabulary stories I used as an example in the section on bottom-up stories (e.g., Mr. White walks. Mrs. White walks . . .)? Now look at Antonio's writing and discuss the same questions. Who used the most correctly spelled words? Now, for the biggest question of all. When I look at Juan's writing, I say to myself, "There is no dog and there is no cat." I know with absolute certainty that Juan is not writing about any living, breathing animal. But I *know* that Antonio is writing about a dog that is very real and that means a lot to him. How do I know this?

When my university students look at these samples, at first they think that, while Juan's writing is impersonal and doesn't convey much of a message (his writing is devoid of *voice*), he is actually a better speller than Antonio. But look again and I think you'll see that this isn't so. Here's why. Juan used only seven words. Yes, they were all spelled correctly. But go back and underline the correctly spelled words in Antonio's story. Don't we see that Antonio used sixteen words that were all correctly spelled *and* he wrote with voice, compared with Juan's seven words that are arranged in a flat, ordered sequence that is devoid of genuine feeling, or what is sometimes called *affect?*

Antonio's story is very cute and all and, yes, he does actually spell more words correctly than Juan, but doesn't allowing kids like Antonio to use incorrect spelling just drill in bad habits and make kids think that cute is better than correct? Isn't this just exactly the sort of warm, fuzzy, cutesy, whole language corruption that scientific educational leaders warn against?

You've identified one of the biggest misconceptions about top-down, meaning-focused teaching. That misconception assumes that because meaning is central and meaning comes first, top-down teachers have an "Oh, well, whatever . . ." attitude and don't bother to teach any skills such as correct spelling, phonics, punctuation, and grammar—or in math, the basic facts. This just isn't true.

There are many ways that a teacher could help bring Antonio to correct spelling. And it's much easier to do this than to convince a child like Juan that writing is about more than assembling words on a page that are spelled correctly—especially since the teacher's actions keep telling him that this is the case.

When you looked at the writing samples, did you conclude that Antonio cares about what he's writing about and Juan cares more about not making a mistake? Look at it this way: Can you imagine a violinist playing only notes that he's already mastered even if it doesn't come together to make a tune? Or can you imagine an athlete practicing only one little skill, say dribbling the ball, and ignoring shooting hoops because he can't do it as well? Of course not. Here are a few of the ways we could help Antonio become a better speller. In fact, his teacher and I worked together and we did use all of these methods, not just for Antonio but for all the other writers in the class, too.

Spelling Method 1
Instead of giving him a list of spelling words that came out of nowhere, we asked Antonio to look at his own work and to think about it. Then we asked him to circle the words he was not sure he spelled correctly. Then as he watched, we wrote the correct spellings on his paper. These then became his spelling words for the week. This isn't as hard as it sounds if younger children start with five words and the number increases as they progress. It's easy to give these little individualized spelling "tests" while the other children are engaged in writing in journals or in writing stories.

Spelling Method 2
We wrote back to Antonio using the words he misspelled. For example, I actually did respond to Antonio's story. I wrote back, "My cat has brown eyes and she's skinny too, like Spotty." In this way, Antonio could see the disconnect between his spelling and conventional spelling. In this class, the children did lots of real reading of real books of their choice, so in addition to explicit instruction targeting spelling and other writing skills, Antonio was also gaining an understanding of how good writing looks and how real language sounds.

This is especially important for the millions of children in our schools for whom English is a second language. Both Juan and Antonio are Hispanic and both had to learn English when they came to school.

Remember Juan's writing and how it reflected the stilted, controlled vocabulary that we see in so many beginning reading basal stories? In other words, what children read affects all their literacy skills. Research shows that the kind of reading kids do is a *model* for their writing. So Antonio's teacher and I made sure we covered all the bases.[82] We gave Antonio lots of opportunities to read and to internalize skills *implicitly*, but we did *not* stop there. We used Antonio's writing to teach skills *explicitly*, too.

That's still pretty fuzzy. How can you be sure that Antonio is even going to notice the difference between his spelling and the correct form that you used?

Here's a question for you: When you're not sure of how to spell a word, what do you do? Most of my students agree that they write out various spelling possibilities. They see which one looks right. Spelling is very visual. Those of us who read a lot and who have lots of exposure to print can usually spot when a word is incorrectly spelled. We see a word, and before we think of any spelling or phonics rule, we think to ourselves, "That looks wrong." We do this because we've read a lot and we've had many opportunities to see and absorb the way language looks. In other words, some skills can be *acquired*.[83]

One more point. I think your question carries with it the assumption that a child is going to look at those words that a bottom-up teacher has circled as being incorrect, see the correct spelling written above it, and actually pause and make a mental note, saying to himself, "Oh, now I get it, it's not *isse*, it's spelled *eyes*. I need to remember that for future reference."

Bottom-up proponents also assume that students will be motivated rather than discouraged by a paper peppered with red marks and that he's thinking—thinking—thinking really, really hard—as he submits to the tedium of copying those words repeatedly. They also assume that a student will stick his head in the buzzsaw again and expand his writing vocabulary even if it's wrong and he knows that he'll be punished for taking a chance by being forced to write incorrectly spelled words repeatedly—to say nothing of getting a bad grade on his paper. Can you see why children who are taught this way would choose to limit the words they use to those that they can spell? When they do so, aren't they giving us a message about what they believe the role of writing is—that it's about the skill instead of about the message?

Also, another important point here. All the spelling rules in the world are *not* going to help in spelling words such as *eyes* and *once* and *there*, to name but a few of the irregularities in our language. Phonics doesn't help here either. But look, I'm not saying that I would **only** write back to children as a way of teaching spelling. Antonio's teacher and I taught spelling in other ways too. Here's an idea that is more explicit and might make you feel a little better about Antonio's future as a good speller.

Spelling Method 3

We asked Antonio's permission to put his letter on an overhead in front of the class. Then I said that his story about his dog reminded me of my cats, and I wrote a funny letter to the class about my cats. I took those words that Antonio and other children misspelled and used them by writing a letter to the class on chart paper, as they watched *and as they helped me sound out the words*. Incidentally, this process of sounding out and matching phonemes (individual sounds) to their respective letters is phonemic awareness. It is phonemic awareness taught as it is actually used.

This method of *shared* writing—not just in front of kids but as they participate—is very important. Think about this. Most of the print we see is already completed. We don't often see someone in the act of writing and have a chance to see how the writing comes down on the paper to create the completed text. Writing in front of the class as the kids help also shows them that letters come down on the page from left to right as well as how all the phonemes and the phonics that bottom-up teaching drills in isolation actually come together to make a message *that makes sense*.

Spelling Method 4

Then, after I'd written the letter about my real cats, I asked the children to circle target words and we talked about them and some of the tricky parts of their spelling. So again, Antonio's teacher and I did teach *explicitly*. When it's possible to do so, we can also use class letters such as this to teach those rules that often work for spelling, such as doubling the final consonant in short words ending in a consonant before adding -*ing*. After writing in front of the students on chart paper, or maybe doing the daily class news on overheads, we spent two minutes typing out our chart paper writing, made copies, and gave them to the class to reread. So, reading, writing, spelling, phonics, and phonemic awareness were taught and taught and taught.

Spelling Method 5

We also asked the class to generate other words that we sometimes misspell and we put them on a word wall so the children could look up and find the words as they were writing. This is a great way—and an authentic way—to teach alphabetical order, too, because we can all discover the need to put those words on the wall in some kind of order so we can find them when we're writing. I've also found that word walls such as this are a great way to ease children into using dictionaries for checking spelling.

Spelling Method 6

We can vary the method of *interactive writing* and give over the pen to the children by working on a class story or a letter on chart paper and leaving blanks for the letters of a missing word. Then we can ask children to say the missing word, pull the sounds out of their mouths, and then come up and write in the letters. In this way, they can see the disconnect between the sounds we hear and the number of letters we write. This is teaching phonemic awareness. And spelling. And phonics. And punctuation, too. And it all starts with meaning and ends with meaning—top down, around, and sideways. That is, what we taught was anchored in meaning at *every* step along the skill ladder. By teaching this way, we did teach spelling as a part of writing and in *many* different ways. All our eggs were not in one spelling program basket.

More important, though, is that our spelling instruction came from the children's own work and they could see the connection to writing and to reading. They had a purpose for using the skill other than "You need to spell correctly so you can pass the spelling test and so that you can get a good job twenty years from now." That "get a good job twenty years from now" argument is meaningless for kids who think they'll live forever and who don't think much further ahead than what they're going to do next weekend. It works for us as adults, but it's just a bunch of words to them. Think about it. Realistically, isn't that true?

But by the time you do all this, children have already misspelled words in their writing. Shouldn't they make sure the words are correct before they write?

As an adult, when you're writing, you may use an occasional word that you're unsure of how to spell. For a minute here, let's just ignore the fact that the spellcheck will alert you to the misspelling and assume that you notice a mistake as you're writing, say, "Ooops," and choose to stop your flow of thought and look up the word in a dictionary right then and there. Fine.

Now imagine you're a child just learning how to write. Most of the words you're writing are ones you're unsure of. So you stop after the first word and look it up, or more likely, you raise your hand and ask the teacher how to spell it. Five minutes later, you move on to the second word, or the third, and you stop again. Do you see the difference in the way a mature writer constructs text and the way a novice approaches it? If a child had to stop after every couple of words to check the spelling, how could she possibly write fluently and remember what she was trying to say? Getting every word right is slow, it is tedious, and it is a great way to discourage kids from writing anything more complex than "I like the dog," as little Juan figured out.

What's more, most authors write and *then* go back and make changes so they can get their ideas down while they're still fresh. Here is a fundamental truth about good writing: In order to write well *and* in order to write correctly, we need a *writing conscience*. That is, we need to care enough to go back and edit our work when there's no teacher around to make us do it. That *caring* has to comes from inside, and it can't be dictated from outside. As teacher Pat Dragon suggests, when we invite children to "write it [their] way," we free them up to think and take chances. Then, we can teach conventions from a piece of work that they actually *care* about.[84]

The idea of teaching skills through writing and connecting writing to lots of reading extends to more advanced writers, too. As children progress and write lengthier stories, top-down teachers devote lots of class time to real writing. They bring in models of their own writing at all stages and at all levels of quality. Then they think through their own pieces in front of the class so that students can see the way a mature writer approaches a task.

Incidentally, I never lie to students by pretending that writing is always fun. I model my attitudes, too. The truth is, I love writing. But I hate it too. Sometimes it's sheer agony. But I let them know that the hard work and the suffering I experience makes me all the more excited when I actually get it to work. I show them my published pieces. I tell them also that bad writing, bad spelling, and sloppy work is rude. It makes my editor have to work a lot harder to fix errors that I should have fixed by myself.

BACK TO THE READING WARS

The difference between bottom-up and top-down teaching—and the heart of the debate over the reading wars—isn't about *if* skills are taught, but *how* they are taught. A top-down teacher does teach those skills, and she can teach them explicitly and directly, but instead of using an inauthentic exercise coming out of nowhere, she uses the writing of a child such as Antonio as an *assessment tool*, and her own stories as a *teaching tool*, so those skills *mean* something to the students' own lives. Then we work from there to teach writing conventions. But we *do* teach them.

And so, we move children to conventional spelling, or grammar, or punctuation while keeping meaning central. Students see how the pieces all fit together. The instruction comes from the students' own work. Students are a part of the process and are active instead of passive. The ideas I've offered here work with kindergarten children, too. I know because I've done it.

I have to make one more point here about one of the major misconceptions that people such as Moats circulate about invented spelling. Somehow, this attack on encouraging children to practice their writing without fear of penalty seems to stem from the notion that children don't *want* to spell correctly. My experience has been this: It's harder to get children to take risks in their writing and to feel as comfortable as Antonio obviously was than it is to get them to spell every word correctly at any cost like Juan did. Kids don't want to make mistakes. They don't want to look stupid, either.

Incidentally, I read the article you mentioned by Louisa Moats on invented spelling in *People* magazine.[85] In it, she that says she herself is not a stellar speller. Then she goes on to blame whole language and the horrors of invented spelling for the collapse of spelling and the alarming level of illiteracy in the nation. I don't understand this, since she is in her late fifties and whole language wasn't even around when she was in school.

What the *People* magazine article doesn't mention is Moats' interest in Sopris West—which publishes the commercial program *Language!*—and her position there as an author as well as the director of research and professional development. Would you agree that there's a lot more money to be made on bottom-up programs than there is on chart paper and overhead transparencies and a classroom full of real books that can be read again and again?

I guess I see your point about teaching writing. But I always thought the reading wars were about how to teach reading, especially phonics. So my question is, how can teachers teach reading skills like phonics from the top down? How can kids read to learn skills when they don't even know how to read?

First, if you go back and think about what we just learned about spelling and writing, not only do you have an idea of the contrasts between bottom-up and top-down approaches to writing skills as they connect to meaning, but you've also seen that writing is a way of teaching phonics and phonemic awareness, too. The teacher starts with where the student is, anchors instruction in meaning, and then teaches *lots* of skills in *lots* of ways. So we taught Antonio not just spelling, not just writing, but also phonics and reading. Remember, our class letter didn't just stop with writing. The children read with us as we wrote it out and we gave them a copy of that letter (or the daily class news) to reread.

Now, let me give you a picture of how to teach other reading skills and phonics. Phonics, as you recall, is the connection between sounds and the letters that produce those sounds.

Reading Aloud and Conversations

The teacher starts with lots of reading out loud to children before they can read themselves. They talk about the stories together in conversation, knee to knee and eye to eye for younger children,[86] and for older children, in conversation groups that look a lot like the book clubs that we enjoy as adults.

The teacher does not ask traditional comprehension questions the way bottom-up teachers do. Instead, she models the kinds of questions that she asks herself as she reads, including what she notices about the language the author uses and words she wonders about and may want look up in a dictionary or ideas she might want to do research on. She also thinks aloud her predictions about what will happen next in a book. And so she's demonstrating for kids what good readers do very naturally and almost unconsciously as they read through texts.[87]

After modeling such as this, students can then use sticky notes to mark their own questions in books as they read themselves. These notes can then be used as the basis for conversations or research projects.

But I've seen basal reading series that ask kids to do predictions and other comprehension activities such as sequencing and explaining cause-and-effect relationships that you talked about in the bottom-up section of this book. Those aren't exclusively top-down methods, are they?

Again, as with skills such as spelling, the difference isn't *if* a skill is taught, but *how* it is taught. Here's what I've seen and what really bothers me about predictions as well as other "comprehension" activities in basal series: They're done as an exercise. In other words, kids need to come up with, say, three predictions about a story and then read and find out if their predictions are accurate.

Is that what you do when you pick up Stephen King or Danielle Steele? Do you think, "Gee. What are three predictions I have about this book? I'll fill out my three predictions on this worksheet that I just happen to have handy and then when I'm finished with the book, I'll go back and fill in the blanks to see if I predicted correctly. Then I'll hand them in to someone to be corrected. This is why I just love reading. Predictions and other worksheets are just so satisfying!"

I doubt that you do that. My guess is that you do make predictions but that you do so very naturally, such as when you're watching a movie and you turn to the person next to you and say, "I'll bet the butler did it," or "I'll bet Clint Eastwood has enough bullets left to make his day." That's what top-down teachers model. They show kids how they really think and react because some kids don't just get that on their own. The difference is that a top-down teacher does it authentically, instead of as some contrived, tedious exercise. That is the beauty of conversations, too. They make thinking fun.

Conversations

When you read, how do you respond to a book, or how do you react to a movie that you've seen with a friend? Do you answer comprehension questions, or do you talk about your impressions with a friend? Even books we don't necessarily like can be fun because we can debate why we don't like them. I do this with my friend Ardie Cole all the time. We often read the same books and see the same movies, but we don't always share the same opinion about what's good and what's not so good. When we debate books, we both need to think hard to crystallize our arguments so the other person can see our point.

Don't we want kids to have that experience too? How can we expect them to learn to organize their thinking and express themselves effectively and politely, too, if we never let them practice those skills, or if we try to control and limit their thinking on worksheets? Also, can you see how conversations, book clubs, and genuine discussions can be a rehearsal for writing well? Doesn't the act of thinking and processing that we do in order to coherently make a point with a friend in conversation relate to what a good writer must do to make his point in a written piece?

Therefore, isn't there a strong connection not just between reading and writing but to conversations, too? Don't authentic opportunities to practice these *language arts* strengthen and support the others? As a rule, good readers are good writers, and they can also express themselves orally because they know how to think and think, and refine and define. They've had lots of practice.

Certainly, there are some questions about books that have right and wrong answers, such as Who did what? But aren't there other parts of reading that are more complex?

Questions for Discussion:　Do we tend to limit comprehension and get kids into habits of shallow, low-level thinking by the ways we control, direct, and assess comprehension traditionally by the use of teacher questions and worksheets? Can comprehension exercises that ask literal, low-level questions such as "Who did what?" actually work against higher-level thinking? Might such exercises actually train kids to think basically and at a bottom level?

One more thought here: Do you realize how few opportunities kids have to participate in genuine conversations? Not the gentle inquisitions of teacher-to-student questioning, not arguments on the playground, not the stilted dialogues that permeate a lot of movies and television, not one-sided lectures and preaching from teachers and parents, but real conversations? At home, a lot of families eat on the run or in front of the TV if they eat together at all. Even in restaurants and bars, the focal point of the room is often a television. In schools, kids sit in separate seats and answer questions devised by the writers of the teacher manuals to be dispensed and evaluated by the teachers.

Questions for Discussion: What is the value of conversation, not only for reading comprehension but as a life skill? How do you learn more—by listening to a lecture, or by actively participating in the process? Which kind of learning sticks—facts or skills that you memorize for a grade or to please a teacher or parent, or skills that carry with them an immediacy, skills that you need to accomplish an important task? Which kind of thinking is deeper?

Again, that sounds all warm and fuzzy. But you still didn't explain how to teach phonics. So you read to kids. So you have conversations. Then what?

Just as there are many ways of teaching skills through writing, top-down teachers teach reading skills in many ways. What we saw with the example I gave of read-alouds is how teachers use the story to help kids understand that reading is about meaning. Conversations, like so many other top-down skills, can come at any point in teaching and in any of the many methods of teaching reading and writing too. Here now is a more explicit way of teaching phonics and other skills.

Shared Reading

In shared reading, the teacher starts with a big book with large print. Or, he may use a poem or a song that is written out on chart paper. He often puts it on an easel so he can point to the words as he reads. The book often has *predictable* text so the children can anticipate the next word that will appear in the text.

For example, here's a sentence from the story *Chicka* Chicka *Boom Boom*, by Bill Martin Jr. and John Archambault.[88] Even if you've never read it, I'll bet you can guess the missing word:

A told B and B told C, I'll meet you at the top of the coconut
_____.

Children can predict the missing word, too. So they read along with the teacher as the teacher points to the words. So right away, they're confident because they think they can read. Kids see that we read from left to right and since the teacher is pointing to the words, they also see that one spoken word equals one written word. They get the very important concept of *speech-to-print correspondence*.

Then, the teacher can go back into the text, as we saw with writing and spelling activities. She can put sentences from the story on sentence strips in pocket charts and do word study— identifying letter combinations and the various sounds they make. In the sample sentence from *Chicka Chicka Boom Boom*, for example, the teacher might look at the combinations of letters that make the long *e* sound in *tree* and brainstorm for other words with the same sound, such as *me, sea, bee, be*. The sounds can then be sorted so kids see that the same sounds can be made with many different letter combinations. The teacher can then reinforce the target sound in a class letter or the daily news. Or he might focus on the *ch* digraph. The possibilities are endless. And the skills instruction is *direct* and *explicit*.

That sounds like it's leaving a lot to chance instead of making sure that phonics is not haphazardly taught but is taught in proper sequence and all the rules are covered.

Well, sad to say, phonics *is* haphazard and there is *no* prescribed sequence for the best way to teach it. Every reading series has its own order of teaching sounds. I think your question also assumes that if we've "taught" a sound, the kids have practiced a sound and can get that sound correct on a worksheet or a test and that they can then apply that sound *and* make sense of print. Life would be a lot easier for all of us if English were nice and regular and if we learned sequentially, but we don't. Sorry, but we don't. Think back to the quotes I took directly from the National Reading Panel report. Didn't we see that the NRP's research showed that when we teach skills in isolation—which is how the panel defined reading and how most of their studies approached reading—kids do not transfer those skills to real text?

Other research supports the evidence the NRP itself gave us on the lack of skills transfer. A researcher out of Harvard, Ellen Langer, did controlled studies on how we learn. She found that skills taught in isolation remain inflexible and are actually invariable.[89] In other words, if we learn a skill in isolation, we can regurgitate it in isolation, but we don't flex our learning easily enough to apply the skill the way we would actually use it.

Isn't this why we use simulators to teach people to fly a plane or perform other important tasks? Brain research also shows that our brains are meaning makers. Our brains value and protect skills that we use while they reject what they consider to be irrelevant. And what makes skills relevant? A need for their use and connections to other skills that we've already mastered, as we saw with reading, writing, listening, and speaking.[90]

Here's an example. I've made many trips by air. I've heard the flight attendants' directions about what to do if we're going to crash dozens of times. Nevertheless, I doubt that I could effectively relate the procedures to you. That information at the beginning of a flight doesn't have much meaning for me. I think most passengers just tune it out, to tell you the truth. But, if our plane were in trouble, I know that every word of those instructions, given as we were going down, would be carved into my brain and I'd have every word memorized before we hit the ground or the water. The relevance of the skill, the immediacy and the authentic need for that skill of what to do when the oxygen masks drop down affect the way that I learn.

Now, keeping that thought in mind, let's get back to your question about what you perceived as the haphazard, take-it-or-leave-it approach that doesn't give phonics the systematic treatment that it deserves. Here are just a couple of examples of why phonics isn't the sort of language system that lends itself to a sequential, rules-bound approach.

Think of the sounds that the letters *ou* make. I can think of these immediately, as we see in the following words: *out, through, though, tough, thorough*. What's the rule that applies? How can we teach kids when the letters *ea* say the sound in *meat* or in *steak* or in *bread*? There is no rule. In fact, most of these examples break the famous "When two vowels go walking, the first one does the talking" rule. The point is, it's really a mistake to communicate the misconception that English is regular. We have to work within the irregularities. If we went through the language piece by piece and sound by sound and exception by exception, drilling all of this into kids or adults who we're trying to motivate into becoming literate, who would want to learn to read?

Furthermore, teachers can structure and control the sounds they want to target by doing word study from big books and by using them in class letters. I know teachers who do have a list of phonics sounds and who are comfortable with checking them off as they're taught and practiced. But they teach those skills in context, and not necessarily in the order that they're listed on that checklist. But they still teach them all. And at least it makes sense and is not as mind-numbingly boring as a sequenced reading series with its endless worksheets and its controlled, one-size, one-sequence-fits-all-kids kind of approach. That approach runs counter to what the government's own studies indicate about how we learn.

Again, getting back to the example you gave of having the kids guess words in sentences, aren't you teaching children bad habits by having them guess words instead of actually reading them? Kids need to know their letters to read words. That is a fact.

First, if you're looking for an argument that kids don't need phonics, you won't get it here. But what we need to look at is what we do when we read. And what role phonics plays in the big picture. It's all very complicated, so now that you're motivated and have a sense of the big picture, let's look at it piece by piece.

Do We Need to Be Taught Phonics in Order to Read?

No. I'm living proof of it, and so are a whole generation of baby boomers who learned to read from the famous Dick and Jane books. The reading method that was in vogue then was called the *sight word method*. I and the rest of that generation using that series were drilled on words that were on flashcards. When we'd memorized the words, we then read the little "See Dick. See Jane. See Spot run" stories. We read these *round-robin* style, where each of us in our little group based on our ability, read our paragraph out loud in turn. I can still remember dreading my turn, counting the kids and matching them to the sentences ahead of me so I could practice my sentences so I wouldn't utterly humiliate myself. In other words, I wasn't paying any attention at all to the other kids' reading, much less the story. The whole agonizing process was all about me.

Dick Allington tells me that there was some small attention to phonics later in the series, although I have no memory of it at all. My first recollection of coming nose to nose with phonics was in my master's program because by then, we were done saving the world with sight words, and all the problems of illiteracy were the result of not enough phonics. I can say that when the sight word method was in vogue, some kids learned to read and some kids didn't. When phonics came back in with a vengeance, some kids learned to read and some kids didn't.

The point is, phonics is not necessary to learn to read. It can help. Sight words help. Lots of immersion in print helps the most. Good libraries and lots of books are essential. But the truth is, some kids cannot hear, much less differentiate among, different sounds, especially if their first language isn't English, because their brains were "programmed" in the phonemic categories of their first language. Here are the NRP report's exact words:

> If teachers have students who are learning English as a second language, they need to realize that their students are almost bound to misperceive some English phonemes because their linguistic minds are programmed to categorize phonemes in their first language, and this system may conflict with the phoneme categorization system in English. . . . Teachers need to know that such children are likely to be confused by instruction in phonics and phonemic awareness. (2-32)

The NRP report goes on to explain that even more confusion occurs when the teachers speak in one regional dialect while the students speak in another. Think of what this means in states like California. I was in a classroom recently where there were fifteen separate first languages that the children spoke, including French, Cambodian, Hmong, Chinese, and Japanese. So when the teacher, who was Latin and spoke with a distinct Spanish accent herself, taught those isolated phonics sounds, most of those kids couldn't even hear some of them, much less distinguish them from one another, much less apply them.

In cases like this, do bottom-up, phonics-heavy programs such as Open Court make sense? For just a minute, forget about the top-down versus bottom-up controversy about how to teach phonics. Does it make sense to rely so heavily on a sound system that kids can't even hear?

Here's one quick example: My daughter's husband is Nepalese, and she's struggled for ten years to learn the language. In Nepalese there are four different sounds for *d* and three different sounds for *t*. For years, not only was Holly unable to articulate those sounds, but she couldn't even hear them. She took her husband's word that they existed and she practiced making those sounds by positioning her tongue in various places in her mouth, but she still has difficulty applying them. It was only when she started to see the different uses in writing that she could begin to see the ways they should be used in speaking. In other words, she needed a context to make sense of it. It's hard to use sounds that you can't even hear or that are used very differently from the sounds in your native language, which are ingrained in your psyche and are second nature to you.

My son-in-law, Birendra, learned English when he was ten years old. He has an exemplary vocabulary. He understands the nuances and subtleties of the language, but he speaks with an accent. He sounds to himself as if he's pronouncing the words the way we do, but he can't hear the differences between what he thinks he's pronouncing and what the rest of us hear. I won't even get into my pathetic attempts to pronounce words in Nepalese. They're a family joke and I'm now forbidden to speak Nepalese to my little granddaughter, Lilia, lest I corrupt her bilingual language development.

In point of fact, the NRP makes two clear recommendations (in the report itself but not in the summary that drives legislation). It calls for balanced reading. It states that phonics is but a tool, a means to an end (2-96). And it warns against heavy phonics instruction with children and teachers with differing dialects. In addition, the NRP also states that children *do* learn phonics and phonemic awareness implicitly through reading and exposure to print.

The problem with dialects and accents is pretty obvious. But it seems to me there's a simple solution. Why couldn't we just train teachers to make the sounds correctly?

Is that really so simple? Let's think about that. Whose dialect or accent would we use as the gold standard of speech? Should we choose a Midwestern accent? This would exclude all present-day Southerners, Westerners, and people from Boston (who don't pronounce their *r*'s) from teaching, much less from training teachers-to-be to lose *their* accents. And once we have a cadre of trainers of phonics with pure accents, of some acceptable origin, how do we fix the problem of all the differing phonemic brain patterns and all the differing accents and dialects of all the different children in all the classrooms in this country? If we were going to select a dialect or an accent as a national standard, it would force millions of people to learn to talk all over again.

While we're at it, do we retrain our public leaders to use a standard dialect, too? Should we retrain people who speak in Texan and southern accents too?

Questions for Discussion: Have you ever had difficulty understanding someone who speaks with a dialect different from your own? Do you agree with the NRP that dialectical differences can confuse children who are learning phonics? Do you believe that our brains are tuned into the phonemic patterns of our original language? Is it possible that mandated phonics programs discriminate against minorities? Why would the government recommend phonics-heavy instruction that goes against its own research findings?

Now, let's move back to top-down and bottom-up teaching of phonics. Which approach offers more variety and covers more bases? Does teaching phonics meaningfully, in context, help students overcome the confusion that might result from differences in dialects between teachers and students?

And now a plea for fairness. Please do not walk away from this book with the idea that I am against phonics. I am not! I'm trying to get us to look at it sensibly, to teach it logically, and to see that it is a tool. Whether we acquire it through reading—as it appears my fellow baby boomers and I managed to do—or through explicit instruction, at some level we do need some phonics. But realistically, phonics is not systematic. And we need to keep a lot of cautions in mind before we buy into some expensive, rigid, bottom-up phonics program hook, line, and sinker.

Come to think of it, maybe training teachers in all the phonemes in a "correct" dialect isn't such a great idea after all. But I need to ask you something. I've seen a lot recently about research about how our eyes move when we're reading and about how our brains light up that proves we read letter by letter, so kids need phonics. How about that? Doesn't that contradict the NRP's own recommendations?

First, let's look at the eye movement research. This research is very important because a lot of the controversy between bottom-up and top-down advocates is centered on what we do when we read. If we read word by word and even letter by letter, as bottom-up advocates claim, then our eyes would not sweep the page. They'd stutter across it with lots of stops. These longish stops, or *fixations*, would prove that the bottom-up people are right and that we read word by word and even letter by letter.

If, on the other hand, we read in chunks, skip over some words, and get meaning from information other than just the letters on the page, then our eye movements would sweep, fixating occasionally on target words.

We have two major approaches to eye movement study. The old eye movement research used a method that held the reader's head in a kind of contraption that kept it from moving. Then the way the reader's eyes moved across the page was tracked. The study used sections of text instead of a large, meaningful piece of text.[91] Even so, the author of one such study did *not* say his findings supported word-by-word, much less letter-by-letter, reading as NRP member Linnea Ehri and Open Court author *and* NRP contributor Marilyn Adams claim.[92]

Now let's look at another eye movement study. I'm very excited about this research. Its author is Peter Duckett, who was a finalist for a prestigious research award for this work.[93] Many of the findings of Duckett's work support the old eye movement study that found we **don't** read word by word. But thanks to new technology, Duckett's study is more sophisticated and expands on the original eye movement study. His study used laser light beams to track what readers did as they read. Thus, the readers' heads weren't locked into a contraption that forced them to move their eyes unnaturally just to be able to see the page.

Duckett found that readers stopped and focused primarily on content words and major meaning carriers. They made significant stops, or fixations, when they got stuck, and they fixated on the most important words, the ones that carry the most meaning—the *content* or *key words*. So Duckett's research shows that we read in chunks and pull all sorts of information systems into the reading process.[94]

I still can't see how you can read without looking at the letters and all the words. It doesn't make any sense to me. I don't really understand all that eye research, and it only confused me.

Activity for Discussion: I think I can give you some examples that will prove to you that you don't read word by word or even letter by letter. Take a blank piece of paper. Now, without looking, turn the page of this book and cover the page with the blank piece of paper. Slide the paper across one sentence, from left to right, but uncover it only one letter at a time. Then, do the same with another sentence, but this time, uncover it one word at a time.

Are you back? Now, do the same little activity revealing three words at a time (be sure you use a different sentence). Next, slide your paper down, line by line. Then remove the paper altogether and read the page following the one you used the paper on. Do you see my point and what Peter Duckett's research proves?

Questions for Discussion: Why was it easier for you to use the largest chunks of text to read? Why was it so annoying (at least I'm assuming it irritated you, too) to read letter by letter or word by word? What message are we giving kids if we make them *fixate* on each letter *always*? Is there a difference between going back and rereading a word and looking carefully at individual letters and looking at every piece—always—as we read?

We don't realize it, but we don't hiccough our way across the text, not if we're good readers, that is. So if we drill kids to read letter by letter, we may well be interfering with their fluency—their ability to read smoothly and accurately and with proper intonation. Furthermore, a lot of mental energy goes into thinking about every piece of the text, so kids may not get to actually figuring out that print needs to make sense.

I have one more little test for you. Have you ever made a mistake as you were reading and said the wrong word? Let's say you read, "A told B and B told C, 'I'll meet you at the top of the coconut *train.*'" What makes you go back and reread that sentence? Just pretend that somehow, you misread that word. You wouldn't miss anything so obvious, but I misread words sometimes and I shake my head, say, "Hey, that doesn't make any sense," and go back and reread and look more carefully at the letters. But, it wasn't getting the letters wrong that cued me in to my error. It was the meaning. What I said didn't make sense.

Incidentally, when I was reading over this section, and I came across the word *misread*, I read it as *misread* in the present tense—you know, *"reeeed"* instead of *"red"*—and I did just what we're talking about. I shook my head and said, "Whoa. That doesn't make any sense," and I went back, reread that word and used the meaning of the whole to get the tense *and* the pronunciation right. I'm wondering if that happened to you when you read that same word. Did it?

There are some words that we just absolutely, positively cannot read without the whole picture, such as *bow* and *read*. Words such as these are absolutely positively impossible to "read" without the meaning of the whole to rely on. It's that whole context that gives us the information and cues us to the meaning, to say nothing of the pronunciation, of the word.

The information that we pull together from the letters and the meaning during that important strategy is called the *cueing systems* because they cue us or nudge us or assist us in reading. We use three main cueing or information systems: (1) We need the meaning of the whole story or text (you can think of it as a kind of *macromeaning* or *semantics*). (2) We also use the meaning of the sentence to help us, particularly to clue us in if we've made a mistake in the tense of a word, as I did with the word *misread*. This cueing system is called the *syntax*. (3) Then of course, we use the letters too. This cueing system is called *graphophonemics*.

These labels sometimes confuse people. Don't be put off by them, though. Just keep in mind the little exercise we did and then when you need to describe the process you used to read efficiently, I think you'll find that the labels come in handy.

Incidentally, Reading Recovery is a program that has been so successful in getting long-term results with problem readers that it has made these terms and this process part of the everyday vocabulary of many teachers. Independent research has shown that the Reading Recovery program that was developed by Marie Clay not only helps kids do better in the short term but gets them out of remedial reading in the long term.[95] In fact, many of its methods are now modified and used by teachers to help all kids learn to read.

Sadly, Reading Recovery is one of the supplemental programs that the government wants to eliminate in favor of regimented commercial programs such as Sylvan Learning and Voyager Learning. As we've seen, the research on Voyager was done by one of its own design team members, Joseph Torgesen.

Here's something else to think about. Isn't this also true? When you're reading and you don't know a word, don't you sometimes just read on anyway and still make sense of the text instead of stopping and deciphering it and maybe looking it up in the dictionary? Why don't you make sure you read every word? How do you make sense out of the text anyway? Isn't it because the meaning of the whole text, the semantics, cues you, clues you, supports you?

If you're thinking that if you had looked at every letter, you wouldn't have made the mistake in the first place, you may be right. But if you were reading letter by letter, would you have been able to make sense out of even that simple sentence from *Chicka Chicka Boom Boom?* Could you make sense of the text when you were doing the paper-sliding exercise letter by letter? I doubt it.

In fact, I think that's one of the reasons that scrolling sign at my bank or across the bottom of a TV screen annoys me so much. It grinds out the words one by one and forces me to read that way. It's unnatural. It's difficult. In real life, we change the pace of our reading. Sometimes we slow down, and that's the right thing to do. Sometimes we speed up, and that's the right thing to do. Teaching kids that fast reading is always better reading is a big, big mistake.

So, now I hope that you can see that Peter Duckett's research actually supports what you have experienced in your own reading. It supports the methods used by Reading Recovery, too. The notion espoused by Linnea Ehri and Open Court author and NRP contributor Marilyn Adams that we should teach kids to focus on the letters instead of meaning actually runs counter to how we want kids to develop as readers. I take that back. It runs counter to how we want them to develop *if* we believe that meaning is the end result of reading and should be included when we use the term *reading growth*.

THE NEED FOR LIBRARIES

In order to get better at reading, it's like anything else. Kids need to practice. They need to read a lot. They need to know that reading is fun, too. And telling them that "The cat sat. The rat spat" is interesting is a lie that they'll soon figure out. If we want kids to be good readers and if we really value reading, then research shows that we need to put our money where our mouths are. We must have real books in our classes and we must give the kids time to practice and to savor reading too. We can still teach skills, of course, but we can't turn reading into a tedious exercise about the letters and the sounds divorced from meaning or relevance, or we will turn kids off to the joy of books instead of motivating them.[96]

But I've heard that the NRP concluded that research shows that independent reading doesn't help kids read better.

Of all the good questions you've asked here, I believe this is the most important. First, the NRP did *not* say that independent reading doesn't help kids. Not at all. What it did say was that there were literally hundreds of studies showing that kids who read more read better.

So, what's the problem then? How did this rumor that the NRP doesn't approve of independent reading get started, anyway?

Remember the reanalysis of the NRP report that Camilli and his team did? Think back and you'll recall that one of the problems he found with the NRP was that it interpreted "rigorous analysis" as meaning "rigorous selection criteria for choosing the studies" instead of rigorous analysis of the studies themselves. There is a big, big difference between paying a lot of attention to the methods a study used and making sure that the study itself looked at what's really important, isn't there?

Another way to put it is that the NRP cared a lot about making sure studies used experimental research—you remember, treatment and control groups? But it fell short when it came to correctly analyzing the content and the outcomes and the practical relevance of those studies. The NRP made a huge, illogical leap. It assumed that the value of studies was that they used experimental research whether or not the actual research was of any pratical value.

Remember, most of that panel consisted of people who weren't classroom teachers. In fact, that fourteen-member "expert reading panel" consisted of a certified public accountant and a physicist, to say nothing of a lot of bottom-up behavioral psychologists who never taught real kids to read in a real classroom. So they just don't get it. Remember, too, that Camilli said that the panel defined *reading growth* as kids' ability to "read" isolated bits and pieces of skills instead of reading real texts and real books. The panel members were "scientists," some of whom had their own bottom-up commercial programs in the works, who sliced and diced a complex process to fit it into the procedures they wanted to use. In other words, the methods of the studies, the panel's own bottom-up biases, and even their financial self-interests may have served to trump the relevance of the studies they looked at.

So the panel claimed that even though there were literally hundreds of studies that showed a relationship between good readers and lots of reading, it wasn't going to include those findings because the studies weren't experimental. Dick Allington makes a good point about why we don't have more studies on independent reading that include treatment groups (in which kids do lots of reading) compared with control groups, where kids just get skills instruction with no opportunity for independent reading.

Allington made this point at a Reading Recovery conference I attended. He asked what parent or principal in his right mind would allow one group of kids to read and demand that a second (control group) not read at all? And while these days, there may well be some principals who think that is a good idea, it would also be impossible to control the reading that kids do at home.

Allington also points out that science can't always rely on experimental research to give us valid and reliable results. Look at the medical profession. If we relied on experimental research to determine the effects of smoking on health, we'd need two groups. One we'd train to smoke from an early age (let's say age ten). Another group, we'd have to police to make sure the individuals didn't smoke at all. Then we'd have to check their health after thirty years or so of smoking or not smoking. Do you see the problem here? Do you see the comparison with the silliness of demanding experimental research to prove reading is good for kids?

Question for Discussion: Dick Allington was part of a research team that studied kids' setbacks in reading.[97] They found that kids who didn't read over the summer—particularly kids in poorer neighborhoods who didn't have much access to books— fell further behind in reading ability than kids who read a lot. What does this study tell us about the need for independent or sustained silent reading in schools? If we buy the panel's claim that "only medical research gives us usable results," then we might as well tell all musicians and athletes to stop practicing because there's no experimental proof that it helps them get better.

One more point: Steve Krashen reanalyzed the NRP data, and guess what? He found that the panel left out studies that should have been included and that when reanalyzed, the findings showed that kids who read more read significantly better.[98]

Again, we need to consider that books that are reusable are much less profitable for entrepreneurial researchers than the programs they have to sell. Of course, we don't know that their financial interests influenced their findings, any more than we know that research done by tobacco companies may be unconsciously shaped by their own self-interests. Think about that a little.

One more question on research. I heard that now they've found the cure for dyslexia and it involves new brain research using something called an MRI that shows that a lot of phonics rewires kids' brains so they can read. You can literally see "the lights come on" as dyslexic kids learn phonics!

I'm going to give you a very insightful analysis of that research by Alis Headlam in a moment. But first, I want to say that in the years I've been in education, dyslexic kids, or kids who have what the promoters of this "'new' approach" call "word blindness," have traditionally been put in special classes. These classes, like a lot of special education programs in schools, rely very heavily on phonics instruction. Letter by letter and sound by sound and word by word. As we've seen, and as Allington points out:

> Given that direct-instruction programs for children identified as learning disabled have been just about the most disastrously unsuccessful educational efforts offered in American schools, it seems almost lunacy that so many of the entrepreneurs of that approach are now offering advice on improving classroom instruction. . . . It would have made sense to me if the politicians had stepped in and eliminated the NICHD and the Office of Special Education and Rehabilitation Services because of their almost complete failure to educate the learning disabled children entrusted to them. But putting the special education direct-instruction gurus in charge of reforming American reading instruction—even Orwell wouldn't have imagined such an outcome.

Now here's what Alis Headlam, who is a Senior Fellow for the Vermont Study of Education, says about this "new" cure for dyslexia in a letter published in the *Rutland Herald* and dated August 6, 2003:

Flawed Solution to Dyslexia

The MRI is being promoted as the newest tool in combating dyslexia. In the July 28 issue of *Time* magazine, "The New Science of Dyslexia" claims to finally provide evidence that teaching discrete elements of text will help dyslexics read. The science is flawed, and the article is misleading as it contradicts itself over and over.

The science is flawed because technology is not as effective as researchers like Sally Shaywitz would have us believe. What readers need to know is that the MRI can only be used to examine very small isolated bits of text and that there is a 20-second delay between the time the stimulus is given and the blood actually flows to a measurable part of the brain. Researchers give subjects a list of pseudo-words to read and then compare that to a list of real words to see if there is a difference in what the brain is doing.

Imagine trying to read "phlat" in the first case and then "flat" in the second case. It isn't clear to those who study neurology what exactly the person is thinking or even focusing on during these experiments, and the 20-second delay makes it even more questionable. How do we know that something other than the text may not be affecting the blood flow? Stress of trying to figure out a non-word, for example, could play a larger part in this than the researchers would have us believe.

The research is misleading because the only "reading" that the subject does is with isolated words. It ignores the fact that all readers depend on the context of print to assist them in decoding words. Without this readers are unfairly compromised. Tests that claim to measure "reading" without context ignore the fact that continuous text with sentences, phrases, and, for young readers, illustrations, help the reader to make sense out of the words on the page and allow him or her to use a variety of strategies. The research in question only looks at the use of phonemic awareness. It concludes that dyslexics need more of this.

However, the *Time* article points out over and over that dyslexic readers need more than isolated bits of text. Dyslexics, the article claims, are better at problem-solving than using "tunnel-visioned, step-by-step sequential" thinking. Why does it then insist that these students use their weakest areas of perception instead of their strongest? When whole meaningful pieces of text are available to readers they can apply their problem-solving skills by using a variety of strategies that include making sense of the text, making it sound like language, making it sound right (pronunciation).

The outcome of research like this one cited in *Time* is used to promote reading programs like the ones being touted by No Child Left Behind legislation. Programs that rely on the systemized teaching of phonics like Open Court and the Wilson Language System are based on the premise that being able to pronounce words is more important than being able to make sense out of text. There is an assumption that children must analyze words before they can construct meaning. This just isn't so. Many children simply can't rely on the pronunciation strategy alone. When text is meaningful it's easier to read.

There is no new evidence to support the notion that dys-lexics or any other readers are better off with programs that limit their reading strategies. Supporters of No Child Left Be-hind don't want to admit this. They don't want to admit that there is research supporting holistic approaches to the teach-ing of reading that needs to be examined. They limit their view to studies that only support their point of view, and they would have us leaving many children behind because they do not have an open mind to the science of education.

Alis Headlam

Two more points about the cure for dyslexia. Sally Shaywitz, author of *Overcoming Dyslexia*, notes that dyslexic children of-ten have other gifts. They tend to be artistic and creative and to see the "big picture." So we need to ask, if we can indeed "re-wire" kids' brains so they see the little bitsy pieces (recall the re-search doesn't show that this method works for the big picture of reading comprehension of connected text), then what part of a child's personality have we sacrificed so she can read letters in isolation and pronounce words on lists? Also, if these kids can see the big picture and this is their strength, then why don't we use that to help them fill in the word blanks? Why rewire them to look at the little picture if that sacrifices their gift for seeing the whole?

The second point: We live in an environment in which we hear "Accountability! Accountability!" Let's hold the people who hammer us with that message accountable themselves. Sup-posedly now, we can nearly cure the crippling disability of dys-lexia. If this brain rewiring that is incidentally being supported and promoted by our federal employee Reid Lyon doesn't work, and we've broken a promise to parents and children that they'll be "cured," then remember this and demand an explanation and a refund.

If my skepticism proves unfounded and we see viable evidence in *real life* and in *real reading* that the cure has been found and dyslexic kids can become readers and appreciators and users of real books and text because someone has rewired their brains, then I'll be the first to apologize and jump on the bandwagon. As it appears to me now, this "new" method is just an old method that hasn't worked before.

HOW DO TEACHING STYLES AFFECT STUDENTS' THINKING AND BEHAVIOR?

A lot of the group activities, conversations, and such in top-down classrooms still sound pretty chaotic to me. My experience tells me that students aren't responsible enough to plan, organize, or work on their own. Not only that, they don't know how to get along with each other and do all the compromising and negotiating that working in groups requires.

A top-down teacher would say that is the point exactly. Students spend more time in school than they do at home. If they spend twelve years, the bulk of their lives, working in isolation and competing with each other, we've turned schools into an artificial environment that doesn't reflect the workplace or the way we are supposed to interact in personal relationships in real life, where compromise and negotiations are necessary and valued. Or, we've actually trained kids to be low-level followers instead of thinkers, doers, and leaders. Some believe that bottom-up classrooms are designed with exactly that goal in mind. For many, that low-level outcome may be entirely unconscious.

But, did you know that traditional classroom settings were originally intended to train students in rote, relatively mindless, "assembly line" activities such as following orders without question and performing routine tasks?[99] Even the physical setting of traditional classrooms, with straight rows of desks, was originally intended to make sure we had a pool of good, low-level service people, taught in the most basic, low-level skills, but who did not think outside the box—much less ask why they were in the box in the first place.

I'm not sure I buy the idea that the climate and the kind of teaching-learning styles of classrooms shape kids into either low-level workers or as you seem to be implying, higher-level, more creative thinkers.

Are you sure? Don't we believe that the home environment shapes kids' values and attitudes? Isn't our goal as parents to help guide our children by encouraging them and building their confidence and belief in themselves? Since kids spend more of their time in school than they do at home, why wouldn't the school setting and the kind of academic training they receive help determine their goals and their belief in what they can accomplish and who they will become? Why wouldn't the physical and social setting of the school influence the way they learn to interact with others—or how they are *socialized?* When you think of it that way, school is a big chunk of the future to entrust to virtual strangers, much less to the government and to businesses who have their own agendas.

Let's think a minute and go back to a question we raised in Section 2 of this book: If businesses and politicians control the schools, whose best interests will they have at heart, their own bottom lines or the interests of our kids? How would the people who want profits and who want to get reelected like to see your children socialized? As thinkers who will challenge the leaders' power or as obedient little robots who will do as they are ordered?

But, as you've pointed out before, schools have traditionally been patterned after that straight-rowed, teacher-centered, worksheet-laden environment. And yet we all learned, and I am successful because of it. So aren't you way off base here?

Child psychiatrist Dr. Robert McKay makes a good point about that. He notes that times have changed.[100] Kids today are bombarded with images from television and movies. Everything is fast and slam-bang and kids are not as willing to sit still for activities that aren't interesting and involving. When you were in school do you ever remember kids who were diagnosed with attention deficit disorder and who needed to be put on Ritalin or other drugs?

Perhaps, if we provided a curriculum that evolved with the times instead of one that was rooted in the past, then we wouldn't have some of the problems we do with dropouts and bad behavior. We'll look more at this question when we discuss the teachers who really influenced and touched you. I'd be willing to bet that they weren't the kind that the government is demanding. More on that later.

Now I'm really confused, because from what I hear, all the new reforms are designed to help our children. I've heard businesses want workers with higher-level skills. Isn't that true?

Hmmm. If you were a businessperson or a politician, would you announce to the world, "I want a pool of workers and/or voters who won't think beneath the surface and challenge me, so I'm pushing this low-level back-to-basics curriculum that makes my workers/voters more manageable," or would you do a PR spin and say, "I support higher standards and a reading curriculum that will save your children and raise their level of literacy"? Would you say, "I want to see privatized schools run by businesses so we can control the way kids think," or would you say, "The public schools are failing. Teachers want us to tell them what to do. We need reform"?

Incidentally, when the last presidential election began, candidate Bush started by attacking public education and calling for the end of it, beginning with the vouchers that we've seen Secretary of Education Rod Paige advocating. That was not popular with teachers or with other voters. So what did candidate Bush do? He changed the rhetoric to one of "reform" but kept the same agenda. Think back. Isn't this true?

A top-down teacher would say that social work-life skills are learned. We can't train kids to perform isolated—some might say mindless—busywork activities for twelve years and then expect them to flip a switch and enter the workplace as thinkers and do-ers with good people skills. Top-down teaching is messy at times, but top-down teachers say, "Yes, it can be messy, but then so is life. So the struggle is well worth it and like anything else, it gets better with practice."[101] So one of the goals of top-down teaching is to set up learning situations that challenge students beyond the basics.

Questions for Discussion: Can you remember teachers you had who excited and challenged you? How many truly memorable teachers have you had? Can you remember classes where you were bored, disengaged, and frustrated? How did the teacher's views of teaching and learning affect your attitudes toward the class? How did the methods and the materials the teacher used reflect your level of interest, motivation, or even inspiration? Into which general teaching style did the bottom-up or top-down teachers fall?

BACK TO THE BEGINNING

Question for Discussion: Way back toward the beginning of this book, I raised the point that NCLB, with its control of the curriculum, was redefining what it means to be a teacher. If you're part of a discussion group, I'd like you to talk to each other about the best teachers you ever had and what made them so memorable.

I can't sit in on your discussion, but I've used this activity in many presentations and in my classes, so the best I can do is give you an overview of what I've learned. Most people say that a good teacher made them feel special, that she or he made learning interesting and engaging, and that she or he managed to set up an environment in which they felt safe and valued. The teacher orchestrated discussions that challenged and even provoked students to think.

Did anyone in your group say that the best teacher he or she ever had did the following?

The best teacher I ever had . . .
- read from a scripted manual
- made me learn every phoneme in the English language
- convinced me phonemes were exciting and got me to cheer for them
- recognized that I didn't need to care about what I was learning and therefore didn't waste time motivating me
- made me practice lots of skills on lots and lots of exciting worksheets
- did not make any decisions on her own because she wasn't smart enough to do so and also because she didn't want to
- taught me the necessary skills to do well on standardized tests as if his very job depended on my performance—which it did

- made sure I kept my thinking at a basic-skills level so I never caused trouble by getting any big ideas on my own
- did not waste my time by forcing me to read books in school
- taught scientifically first and foremost

I know that at first glance, this list sounds like a rather flip attack on the new legislation and the mandated reading programs such as Open Court. But do me a favor, please. Look at that list again and tell me which item on that list is not part and parcel of the new education reforms. What these reforms bode for us is a redefining of what it means to be a teacher as well as what it means to be a learner. I hope you'll leave this book thinking and questioning methods, materials, research, and buzzwords. Now, I'll answer your final questions and we'll wrap this up in the last section of this book.

Section VIII

WHAT CAN WE DO ABOUT IT?

You raise a lot of important points here, but I think what you present is a very cynical view of research and our government. Wouldn't you agree?

No, I don't agree at all. As a matter of fact, I'm very much an idealist and an optimist, too. I believe in our Constitution and that we have not just a right but a *responsibility* to challenge our government and to have a voice in who our children become. If I were a cynic I'd just throw up my hands and give up instead of trying to help teachers and parents and legislators wake up to the realities of current "reforms" and see who's hiding behind that curtain of buzzwords such as *accountability* and *standards* and *No Child Left Behind*. I'd just let the Wizards take over the world and our children, and I'd sit back and shake my head at the spectacle. But I truly believe in the ideals and the values of our democracy. I won't give that up without a fight.

Way back in the beginning of the book, I asked you how we could know that we can trust you. Now that we know you better, how do we know that you're not just another Wizard?

Much of what I've presented here meets those Wizards on their own ground. In other words, for the most part, I didn't pull a lot of counterresearch out of a hat and get into a "this says–that says" research debate. I used the government's own research data and its own words to show that even though these Wizards made up all the rules and broke nearly every one of them, they still couldn't support their own reforms based on their very own facts. Think back. While my arguments are passionately presented, as I

147

freely admit, do you see many that aren't based on the government's own words and actions?

But don't you have a lot at stake here, too? After all, aren't you interested in selling this book even though you have a lot to say about the financial agendas of others?

Oh, my. There are several very basic differences between those big-time Wizards and me. First, anyone can choose to buy or not buy this little book. Even if people do, realistically, I'll be lucky if it gets into the hands of a couple thousand teachers and even a hundred parents, and maybe—just maybe—a mere handful of legislators will actually read it. That's if I'm really, really lucky.

Contrast this to government-mandated programs that force the sale of millions and millions of basal readers and supplemental programs and push them into the hands of every single child in this country. Anyone has a choice to buy or to not buy my book, assuming they ever even hear of it, which they probably won't. Contrast my little book's chances of hitting the *New York Times'* best-sellers list to a book written by one of the entrepreneurial "scientific research" Wizards, who can use the government's own public relations machine.

I know the government game here. If my agenda were to make a lot of money and get into a position of power, then don't you think I'd be on that bandwagon, writing about the glories of the great "science" and touting the federal initiatives so that I could benefit from a recommendation of, say, Reid Lyon or Edward Kame'enui or Louisa Moats or Rod Paige? I've never worked for a basal reading publisher in any way, shape, or form. I'm going out on a limb to make a prediction here: I predict I will never be a recipient of the prestigious McGraw-Hill Educator of the Year Award.

What if you're wrong about all this?

I've given you lots of research as well as many opportunities to answer that question within this book. But *if* I'm wrong, what is the impact of my mistaken notions? You've read a book that's provoked you into thinking and defending your own beliefs. That's all. I don't make federal or local policy, and what's more, I wouldn't if I could. My whole point is that you as teachers and parents **own that right,** and while I have done what I could to persuade you, the decisions you make are none of my business after all. I have no power, and if I'm wrong (and I'm not), then no harm done really.

Now turn that around. You have a lot of evidence in this book to show that *they*—the experts and the Wizards who control our schools—are wrong. A better question is What if Garan's right and *they're* wrong? Then what? Think about it.

What you present here is very troubling. But what can any of us do about it?

First and foremost, as I said in the section on stress and competition, define and clarify your own values. It's not my business to tell you what to do or how to think. It is my business, though, to share with you what I know about all this because I really believe many teachers and most parents have no idea what this "reform" means for schools and kids. I always tell audiences that when we clarify what we believe in, then we need to draw a line and say, "This is what I believe. This is what I can't give up." Once you've done that, stick to it. Everyone's line is different. Find your own line and when you do, here are some suggestions to help you hold that line and hold on to your power and the power of your children's future.

Smart Action You Can Take to Help Kids

- If you're a parent, be there. Be at that school. Open and maintain a dialogue with your child's teacher and with the school board as well. Don't—don't—**don't** be afraid to speak up and do **not** be silenced or intimidated. You can't afford to.
- Organize with other parents and teachers. You need support. When you speak up, it's good to have a little posse there to cheer you on. Everyone is more comfortable speaking out when he knows he's not alone.
- Form discussion groups around books, issues, and websites on education. Then take action. Write letters protesting standardized and bad educational policies. Be visible and vocal at school board meetings as a *concerted* force.
- Highlight the sections in this book explaining the smoke and mirrors and **have your facts at hand.**

- Use your state and local reading councils to set goals and take action for advocacy. Keep dialogues open and keep abreast of current developments and what is happening in other states in the implementation of mandates. It also helps to get on Internet forums and to dialogue with others. We have been isolated and silenced. We need to get unisolated.
- Use your unions. While not all of us may agree totally with everything that unions do, they do have a national presence and political clout. Use that clout to fight the deskilling of teachers and corporate takeovers.
- California Reading Association has hired a lobbyist to make our voices heard. We, the professionals, have been excluded from the decision-making process. We need to advocate for our profession and for children instead of allowing people who have never taught to set the goals for us.
- Recognize that the climate has changed and that we can no longer just sit back and ride out the latest wave of political and financial pressure. This is not business as usual.
- When we read an attack on the schools in the papers or hear it in the media, we must respond. Ask, "How do you know that? What evidence do you have to support that claim? What is the source of that evidence? How do you know that is true? What underlying motives may drive the source you used to report this information? Who stands to profit financially from this claim?" We need to provide counterevidence and respond. More importantly, we need to get *them* to start questioning and to assume their share of all that accountability they advocate for *us*.

There is one more thing you can do that will help. Take one dollar (or more), put it in an envelope, and send it to

The World of Opportunity
7429 Georgia Road
Birmingham, AL 35212

Why should I do that?

Because there are teachers and parents who want to do something to help fight the high-stakes testing, the federal mandates, and all the rest of the "reforms," but they are scattered and don't have the time or the means to get organized in a big way. WOO is a little group that *is* organized and helps kids in lots of ways. It helps those kids who were pushed out of school and it campaigns and lobbies to fight high-stakes testing and mandates. This is a nonprofit organization, so your one dollar (or more) is tax deductible. Susan Ohanian reads all the notes she receives and she shares them with many of the kids the WOO helps so they can see all the people who cared enough to do this. My mom sent money and so did my daughter in my little granddaughter's name. I'm quite proud of that.

One last question. Many teachers are discouraged to the point of despair. In fact, many wonderful teachers are leaving the profession. Do you have any final words of encouragement to keep us from giving up?

Yes. Watch *Seabiscuit*.

REFERENCES

Adams, Marilyn Jager. 1990. *Beginning to Read: Thinking and Learning About Print*. Cambridge, MA: MIT Press.

Adams, Marilyn Jager, et al. 2002. *Open Court Reading*. DeSoto, TX: McGraw-Hill.

Adams, Marilyn Jager, Barbara Foorman, Invar Lundberg, and Terri Beeler. 1997. *Phonemic Awareness in Young Children: A Classroom Curriculum*. New York: Paul H. Brookes.

Allington, Richard. 2002. *Big Brother and the National Reading Curriculum: How Ideology Trumped Evidence*. Portsmouth, NH: Heinemann.

Allington, Richard, and A. M. McGill-Franzen. 2001. The Impact of Summer Reading Loss on the Reading Achievement Gap. Paper presented for publication.

Allington, Richard, and Haley Woodside-Jiron. 1998. "Decodable Text in Beginning Reading: Are Mandates and Policy Based on Research?" *ERS Spectrum: Journal of School Research and Information* 16 (Spring): 3–11.

Amrein, Audrey, and David Berliner. 2002. "High-Stakes Testing, Uncertainty, and Student Learning." *Education Policy Analysis Archives* 10 (18). 28 March. Accessed at <*epaa.asu.edu/epaa/v10n18/*>.

Bowie, Liz. 2002. "Edison Fails to Improve Two Schools." 30 January. Accessed at <*www.sunspot.net/bal-md.edison30jan30.story*>.

Boucher, Derek. 2003. "Reading Programs Mean Big Money for Big Business." Letter in the *Fresno Bee*, 14 June.

Brown, W., E. Denton, P. Kelly, and J. C. Neal. 1999. "Reading Recovery Effectiveness: A Five-Year Success Story in San Luis Coastal Unified School District." *ERS Spectrum: Journal of School Research and Information* 17: 3–12.

Buck, Julie, and Joseph Torgesen. 2003. The Relationship Between Performance on a Measure of Oral Reading Fluency and Performance on the Florida Comprehensive Assessment Test. FCRR Technical Report No. 1. Tallahassee, FL: Florida Center for Reading Research.

Byron, Christopher. 2002. "Edison Schools Flunk." 6 May. Accessed at <*www.nypost.com/business/47263.htm*>.

Camilli, Gregory, Susan Vargas, and Michele Yurecko. 2003. "Teaching Children to Read: The Fragile Link Between Science and Federal Education Policy." *Education Policy Analysis Archives* 11 (15). 8 May. Accessed at <*epaa.asu.edu/epaa/v11n15/*>.

Ceprano, Maria, and Elaine Garan. 1998. "Emerging Voices in a University Pen-Pal Project: Layers of Discovery in Action Research." *Reading Research and Instruction* 38 (1): 31–56.

Cole, Ardith. 2003. *Knee to Knee, Eye to Eye: Circling in on Comprehension*. Portsmouth, NH: Heinemann.

Cunningham, Patricia, and Richard Allington. 2003. *Classrooms That Work: They Can ALL Read and Write*. 3d ed. Boston, MA: Pearson Allyn and Bacon.

Dragon, Pat Barrett. 2001. *Literacy from Day One*. Portsmouth, NH: Heinemann.

Duckett, Peter. 2002. Finalist for the Outstanding Dissertation Award presented by the International Reading Association.

———. "Reading as a Systemic Process: What the Eye Movements of Six Year Old Beginning Readers Tell Us." Unpublished dissertation.

Ehri, Linnea, Bruce McCandliss, Dolores Perin, Hollis Scarborough, Sally Shaywitz, Joanna Williams, Joanna Uhry. 2003. Letter to New York City School Chancellor Joel Klein and others. 4 February.

Ehri, Linnea, and S. Stahl. 2001. "Beyond the Smoke and Mirrors: Putting Out the Fire." *Phi Delta Kappan* 83 (1): 17–20.

Foorman, Barbara, and Jack Fletcher. 2003. "Correcting Errors." *Phi Delta Kappan* 84 (9): 719.

Fuller, Ben. 2003. "Survey: Teachers See Selves as Scapegoats." Press release from the Associated Press. 3 June. Accessed at <*www.seattlepi.com*>.

Garan, Elaine. 1994. "Who's in Control? Is There Enough 'Empowerment' to Go Around?" *Language Arts* 71 (3): 192–9.

———. 2001a. "Beyond the Smoke and Mirrors: A Critique of the National Reading Panel Report on Phonics." *Phi Delta Kappan* 82 (7): 500–6.

———. 2001b. "What Does the Report of the National Reading Panel Really Tell Us About Teaching Phonics?" *Language Arts* 79 (1): 61–70.

————. 2002. *Resisting Reading Mandates: How to Triumph with the Truth.* Portsmouth, NH: Heinemann.

Gendar, Alison. 2003. "City Tells W It's Hooked on 'Phonics'." *New York Daily News.* 25 January. Accessed at <*www.nydailynews.com*>.

Glaser, Janice-Kiecolt, and Ronald Glaser. 2003. "Why Stress Kills." 30 June. Washington, D.C.: Proceedings of the National Academy of Sciences.

Glovin, David. 1998. "Low-Paid Part Timers Judge N. J. Students." *The Record of Hackensack, New Jersey.* 28 November: 12.

Good, R. H., R. A. Kaminski, S. Smith, D. S. Simmons, E. J. Kame'enui, and J. Wallin. In press. "Reviewing Outcomes: Using DIBELS to Evaluate a School's Core Curriculum and System of Additional Intervention in Kindergarten." In *Reading in the Classroom: Systems for Observing Teaching and Learning,* ed. S. R. Vaughn and K. L. Briggs. Baltimore: Paul H. Brookes.

Good, R. H., D. S. Simmons, E. J. Kame'enui, R. A. Kaminski, and J. Wallin. 2002. Summary of Decision Rules for Intensive, Strategic, and Benchmark Instructional Recommendations in Kindergarten Through Third Grade. Technical Report No. 11. Eugene, OR: University of Oregon.

Goodman, Kenneth, Patrick Shannon, Yvonne Freeman, and Sharon Murphy. 1988. *A Report Card on Basal Readers.* New York: Richard C. Owen.

Goodnough, Abby. 2002. "After Disputes on Scoring, School System Switches Provider of Reading Tests." 28 September. Accessed at <*www.nytimes.com/2002/12/28/education/28EXAM.html?todaysheadlines*>.

Greene, Jane Fell. 1996. "*Language!* Effects of an Individualized Structured Language Curriculum for Middle and High School Students." *Annals of Dyslexia* 46: 51–76.

Hall, Dorothy, Patricia Cunningham, and Chris McIntyre, eds. 2002. *Month-by-Month Phonics for First-Grade.* Greensboro, NC: Carson Dellosa.

Headlam, Alis. 2003. "Flawed Solution to Dyslexia." Letter published in the *Rutland Herald,* 6 August. Accessed at <*www.rutlandherald.com/columns/articles/69738.html*>.

Helfand, Duke. 2002. "Teens Get a Second Chance at Literacy." *Los Angeles Times*, 21 July. Accessed at <*www.latimes.com/news/local/la-me-read21jul21005056*>.

————. 2003. "State Reading Scores Remain Dismal." *The New York Times*, 19 June.

Hirsch, E. D. 1987. *Cultural Literacy: What Every American Needs to Know*. New York: Houghton Mifflin.

How the Brain Learns. 1998. Themed issue of *Educational Leadership* 58 (3): ASCD.

Jensen, Eric. 1998. *Teaching with the Brain in Mind*. Alexandria, VA: ASCD.

Juettner, Virginia. 2003. External Facilitator and Evaluator for School Improvement, State of Alaska. In an interview, 13 August.

King, Stephen. 2002. *On Writing: A Memoir of the Craft*. New York: Pocket.

Kohn, Alfie. 2000. *The Case Against Standardized Testing: Raising the Scores and Ruining the Schools?* Portsmouth, NH: Heinemann.

Krashen, Stephen. 1993. *The Power of Reading: Insights from the Research*. Englewood, CO: Libraries Unlimited.

————. 2001. "More Smoke and Mirrors: A Critique of the National Reading Panel Report on Fluency." *Phi Delta Kappan* 83: 119–23.

————. 2002. "Whole Language and the Great Plummet of 1987–92: An Urban Legend from California." *Phi Delta Kappan* 83 (10): 748–53.

Lamott, Anne. 1994. *Bird by Bird: Some Instructions on the Writing Life*. New York: Pantheon.

Langer, Ellen J. 1989. *Mindfulness*. Cambridge, MA: Perseus.

Lewin, Tamar, and Jennifer Medina. 2003. "To Cut Failure Rate, Schools Shed Students." *The New York Times*, 31 July.

Manzo, Kathleen Kennedy. 2003. "Analysis Calls Phonics Findings into Question." *Education Week*, 21 May.

Martin, Bill Jr., and John Archambault. 1987. *Chicka Chicka Boom Boom*. New York: Simon and Schuster.

Martinez, T., and A. Martinez. 2002. "Texas-Style Education Works Against Hispanics." *The Houston Chronicle*, 20 September. Accessed at <*www.houstonchronicle.com*>.

McKay, Robert. 2003. "On Cultural Amnesia." Letter in the *Philadelphia Inquirer*, 14 July.

Moats, Louisa. 2000. "Whole Language Lives On." October. Accessed at <*www.edexcellence.net/library/wholelang/moats.html*>.

———. 2002. "Why Can't Johnny Spel?" *People Weekly*, 27 August: 111–12.

Neal, J. C., and P. R. Kelly. 1999. "The Success of Reading Recovery for English Language Learners and Bilingual Students in California." *Literacy Teaching and Learning: An International Journal of Early Reading and Writing* 4: 81–108.

Neuman, Susan, and D. Celano. 2001. "Access to Print in Low-Income and Middle-Income Communities." *Reading Research Quarterly* 36 (Jan/Feb/Mar): 8–26.

No Child Left Behind. 2002. Accessed at <*www.ed.gov/index.jsp*>.

Ohanian, Susan. 1999. *One Size Fits Few: The Folly of Educational Standards*. Portsmouth, NH: Heinemann.

Paige, Rod. 2002. Letter to the Honorable Patricia Schroeder. 5 April. Accessed at <*www.ed.gov/policy/elsec/guid/letter/020910.html?exp=0*> or type in these search terms: Paige Schroeder September 10.

———. 2003. "Where's the Choice"? Letter in the *Wall Street Journal*, 29 July.

PEN Weekly NewsBlast. 2003. "Teachers Union Softens Stance Against No Child Left Behind Law." *Public Education Network*, 11 July. Accessed at <*www.publiceducation.org/viewnewsblast.asp?id=101&date=7/11/2003*>.

Police, The. 1983. "Every Breath You Take." *Synchronicity*. A and M sp=3735.

Public Agenda. May 2003. Survey: What Teachers Really Think About Unions, Merit Pay, and Other Professional Matters. Available at <*www.publicagenda.com*>.

Rayner, K. 1981. "Eye Movements and the Perceptual Span in Reading." In *Neuropsychological and Cognitive Processes in Reading*, ed. F. Pirozzolo and M. Wittrock. New York: Academic.

————. 1997. "Understanding Eye Movements in Reading." *Scientific Studies of Reading* 1 (4): 317–39.

Reading First. Accessed at <*www.ed.gov/index.jsp*>.

Report of the National Reading Panel: Teaching Children to Read: Report of the Subgroups. 2000. Washington, D.C.: National Institute of Child Health and Human Development.

The Report of the National Reading Panel: Teaching Children to Read: Summary Booklet. 2000. Washington, D.C.: National Institute of Child Health and Human Development. Accessed at <*www.nationalreadingpanel.org*>.

Reuters. 2002. "Calif. Energy Lawsuit Alleges Phony Trading Data." *New York Stock Exchange Newsletter*, 22 November.

Rogers, Fred. 2001. Commencement address at Middlebury College, Vermont, May.

Routman, Regie. 2003. *Reading Essentials: The Specifics You Need to Teach Reading Well*. Portsmouth, NH: Heinemann.

Rowling, J. K. 2003. *Harry Potter and the Order of the Phoenix*. New York: Scholastic.

Sarason, Seymour. 2004. *What Do You Mean by Learning?* Portsmouth, NH: Heinemann.

Schemo, Diana. 2003. "Education Secretary Defends School System He Once Led." *The New York Times*, 26 July.

Shanahan, Timothy. 2001. "Response to Elaine Garan." *Language Arts* 79 (1): 70–71.

————. 2003. "Research-Based Reading Instruction: Myths About the National Reading Panel Report." *The Reading Teacher* 57 (7): 646–56.

Shannon, Patrick. 1989. *Broken Promises: Reading Instruction in the Twentieth-Century*. Boston, MA: Bergin and Garvey.

Shaywitz, Sally. 2001. Videotape of "A Blueprint for Professional Development for Teachers of Reading and Writing: Knowledge and Skills." Symposium on the National Reading Panel Report and Teacher Preparation: UCOP/CPDI, 27 October.

————. 2003. *Overcoming Dyslexia: A New and Complete Science-Based Program for Overcoming Reading Problems at Any Level*. New York: Knopf.

Torgesen, Joseph. 1998. "Catch Them Before They Fall: Identification and Assessment to Prevent Reading Failure in Young Children." *American Educator/American Federation of Teachers*, Spring/Summer.

Wilde, Sandra. 2002. *Testing and Standards: A Brief Encyclopedia.* Portsmouth, NH: Heinemann.

Willson, Meredith. 1957. "Ya Got Trouble." From *The Music Man.*

Winerip, Michael. 2003. "Rigidity in Florida and the Results." *The New York Times*, 23 July. Accessed at <*www.nytimes.com/2003/07/23/education/23EDUC*>.

Winter, Greg. 2002. "Make-or-Break Exams Grow, But Big Study Doubts Value." *The New York Times*, 28 December. Accessed at <*www.nytimes.com/2002/09/28/education/28EXAM*>.

Yatvin, Joanne. 2000. "The Report of the National Reading Panel: Minority View." Accessed at <*www.nationalreadingpanel.org*>.

———. 2002. "Babes in the Woods: The Wanderings of the National Reading Panel." *Phi Delta Kappan* 82 (5): 364–69.

NOTES

SECTION I: SCHOOLS, WIZARDS, AND PULLING BACK CURTAINS

1. Garan 2002.

2. Krashen 2001. Steve Krashen first used the term *urban legend* in reference to the manipulation of the NAEP scores.

SECTION II: BEHIND CURTAIN NUMBER 1: SCHOOL "REFORM"

3. From the song "Every Breath You Take" by The Police.

4. *Newsweek* June 6, 2001, and June 10, 2001. Articles by Joe Horn. If you want the stories, go to Google and type in "Sony + Vertical Limit." You can also access at <*cinema.com*> Vertical Limit, News, "Sony Suspends Studio Executives Over Bogus Critic," June 10, 2001.

5. Fuller 2003. The study that the article reviews is "Stand by Me: What Teachers Really Think About Unions, Merit Pay and Other Professional Matters." It's available at <*www.publicagenda.com*>.

6. Byron 2002.

7. For the Voyager website, go to <*www.voyagerlearning.com*>.

8. The Voyager Learning website lists its design team members and Torgesen's research.

9. Lyon, Reid. November 18, 2002. At this time you can still see Reid Lyon making this statement on a video webcast at <*www.excelgov .org/displayContent.asp?Keyword=prppcEvidence*>. Go to his name and click on the "View Webcast" link. It opened into Real Player on my computer. Lyon is the second person to talk in the panel and the statement is about a third of the way into the video.

10. You can access the document in its entirety on the Web. Go to <*www.ed.gov/nclb/landing/jhtml*> or just type "No Child Left Behind" into a search engine. For a different viewpoint on the legislation, go to <*www.susanohanian.org*>.

11. Sarason 2004.

12. Ibid.

13. Ibid.

14. Paige 2002.

15. Paige 2003.

16. I owe the ideas in this segment to Joanne Yatvin.

17. PEN Weekly NewsBlast for July 11, 2003.

18. Juettner 2003.

SECTION III: BEHIND THE CURTAIN OF ACCOUNTABILITY: ALL ABOUT TESTING

19. Rowling 2003, 243.

20. Willson 1957.

21. Wilde 2002.

22. Kohn 2000, 19.

23. Ibid., 14.

24. Kohn 2000.

25. Goodnough 2002.

26. King 2002.

27. Glovin 1998. Cited in Kohn 2000, 12.

28. Kohn 2000.

29. Hirsch 1987. Cited in Ohanian 1999.

30. Winerip 2003.

31. Brown et al. 1999. In addition to longitudinal studies, other independent measures such as data collection and monitoring have established long-term success for students in Reading Recovery. That is, once they are tutored, they reenter the school setting successfully and they maintain that success.

32. See <*www.voyagerlearning.com*>.

33. *Report of the National Reading Panel* 2000. Later we will examine the discrepancies between the *Report of the Subgroups* and the short, separate *Summary Booklet*.

34. Krashen 2001. Also see Neuman and Celano 2001.

35. Amrein and Berliner 2002.

36. Winter 2002.

37. Helfand 2003.

38. Amrein and Berliner 2002.

39. For information on the hidden student dropout rates in Texas, see Martinez and Martinez 2002 and Schemo 2003. For information on New York City's "invisible" dropouts, see Lewin and Medina 2003.

40. Lewin and Medina 2003.

SECTION IV: A HARD LOOK AT STRESS AND COMPETITION

41. Glaser and Glaser 2003.

42. Jensen 1998. See also *How the Brain Learns*, a themed issue of *Educational Leadership*.

43. Rogers 2001.

SECTION V: BOTTOM-UP TEACHING, METHODS, MATERIALS, AND RESEARCH

44. Allington 2002.

45. Helfand 2002.

46. *Report of the National Reading Panel* 2000, 2-90. *Note:* There are at least three different versions of this report. None is marked by edition, nor is there any record of the changes in ordering of information. Therefore, your page number may not match the information given here. This is an ongoing frustration for those of us who try to make sense of and cross-check information in this "scientific" research study.

47. Visit the Sopris West website at <*www.sopriswest.com*>. There you can also get Moats' email address and see her author biography. *louisam@sopriswest.com*

48. Cunningham and Allington 2003.

49. Moats 2000.

50. Goodman et al. 1988.

51. Paige 2002.

SECTION VI: GOVERNMENT-APPROVED PROGRAMS, METHODS, AND THE RESEARCH CLAIMS

52. Letter dated February 4, 2003, to New York City School Chancellor Joel Klein. The letter is signed by Linnea Ehri, Bruce McCandliss, Dolores Perin, Hollis Scarborough, Sally Shaywitz, Joanna Williams, and Joanna Uhry. Three of the authors are members of the National Reading Panel: Ehri, Williams, and Shaywitz, who now claims to have found the cure for dyslexia.

53. Moats 2000. The claim that teachers do not want to make decisions is repeated in the Ehri et al. letter to New York City school officials. That letter states that Month-by-Month Phonics is not approved by these panel members, who also "are serving on committees at the federal level involving the No Child Left Behind legislation." The letter continues that MM Phonics "places an unrealistic burden on teachers for making decisions. . . ." Apparently, only a privileged few should be making decisions for schools.

54. Boucher 2003.

55. NRP report. Study 11. See Table G.

56. NRP report. See also Garan 2002 for a more detailed description of the NRP results for various commercial programs.

57. Camilli et al. 2003.

58. Manzo 2003.

59. Shanahan 2003.

60. *Report of the National Reading Panel* 2000, 2-84. Disabled readers were generally identified as those children who showed a discrepancy between their IQ's and their reading ability. Their problem was reading-specific. *Low-achieving* readers were identified as children performing lower than expected and who generally were of normal intelligence.

61. The five NRP members or contributors who admit the summary doesn't match the findings are Shanahan 2001; Yatvin 2002; Ehri and Stahl 2001; and Foorman (Foorman and Fletcher 2003). Incidentally, *after* Ehri admitted that the summary lacked the necessary qualifiers and "details," she repeated the summary statement that the NRP concluded that "phonics significantly benefits all children in grades K–6" at a symposium in Los Angeles in October 2001. In other words, rather than correcting the errors, she perpetuated them. I have the entire symposium on videotape, as tapes were sent to all California State University reading faculty so that we would be sure to teach scientifically.

62. Foorman and Fletcher 2003.

63. See <*www.nationalreadingpanel.org*>. Click on "Press Releases and Testimony," then on "Press Releases."

64. Yatvin 2002.

65. Shaywitz 2001.

66. Foorman and Fletcher 2003.

67. Ibid.

68. Adams 1990.

69. NRP report. Table G.

70. Adams et al. 1997.

71. Go to <*www.sopriswest.com*>.

72. Boucher 2003. Fresno teacher Derek Boucher attended *Language!* training for six hours a day for an entire week. He took notes.

73. Greene 1996.

74. Press release, April 10, 2000. Available at <*www .nationalreadingpanel.org*>.

75. Business Wire. January 23, 2001. Washington. Press release.

76. This information is available at <*www.whitehouse.gov/ government/paige-bio.html*>. He was introduced as the recipient of this

honor when he spoke at the International Reading Association conference in May 2001.

77. The endorsements are available on the Voyager website and
are part of its advertising brochure. See <*www.voyagerlearning.com*>.

78. City   Limits   <*www.citylimits.org/content/articles/weeklyView.
cfm?articlenumber=820*>.

79. The Voyager design team and the research supporting it are at
<*www.voyagerlearning.com*>.

80. The research supporting DIBELS conducted by the Voyager
design team as well as those with interests in the program can be
found in Buck and Torgesen 2003; Good, Kaminski, Smith, Simmons,
Kame'enui, and Wallin (in press); and Good, Simmons, Kame'enui,
Kaminski, and Wallin 2002.

81. Allington 2002.

SECTION VII: TOP-DOWN TEACHING, METHODS, MATERIALS, AND RESEARCH

82. Ceprano and Garan 1998.

83. Krashen 1993. See also Neuman and Celano 2001.

84. Dragon 2001.

85. Moats 2002.

86. Cole 2003.

87. Cunningham and Allington 2003.

88. Martin and Archambault 1987.

89. Langer 1989.

90. Jensen 1998.

91. Rayner 1997.

92. Ehri 1996. See also Adams 1998.

93. Peter Duckett was a finalist for the International Reading
Association Outstanding Dissertation Award for 2002. Peter Duckett
has a book contracted with Heinemann tentatively titled, *All Eyes on
Reading*.

94. Duckett. Unpublished dissertation.

95. Brown et al. 1999.

96. Routman 2003. See also Krashen 1993.

97. Allington and McGill-Franzen 2001.

98. Krashen 2001.

99. Shannon 1989.

100. McKay 2003.

101. Garan 1994.

INDEX

abridged reading materials, 76
accountability, as buzzword, 1, 12, 18, 21, 28, 29–30
ACT scores, 50
Adams, Marilyn, 87, 102, 105, 132
advocacy, activism, 3, 6–7, 65, 147–50
Alaska, impact of NCLB legislation in, 27
Allington, Richard, 109, 129, 137–38
alphabetical order, 119
"alternatives," as buzzword, 12
Archambault, John, 126
assessment, 32
authority, importance of questioning, 4–7
average scores (standardized tests), implications, 30, 43–46

back-to-basics teaching methods, 1, 21
balanced reading, 130
Barbara Bush Foundation, 105
basal readers, reading programs, 71–72, 78–80, 83–84, 123
baseline performance, 43
Beeler, Terri, 102
Beginning to Read report, 102
bell-shaped curve (normal distribution), 44
Berliner, David, 50
Best, Randy, 106
"bipartisanship," as buzzword, 12, 15
bilingual education, 50
bottom-up classrooms, methods, 68–77, 87–88, 92–94, 117, 127, 142–44. *See also* No Child Left Behind legislation
Boucher, Derek, 86–87
bullying, 60
Bush, George W. *See* No Child Left Behind legislation
Bush, Jeb, 45, 107
Bush, Neil, 107
buzzwords, as education policy, 18–19

California, impact of NCLB legislation in, 50–54, 81
Camilli, Gregory, 95–96
Carnine, Douglas, 107
cause and effect studies, 69, 76
Chicka Chicka Boom Boom (Martin, Jr. and Archambault), 126
child-to-child comparisons, 34, 43
chunked reading, 132–33
citizen participation, 6–7, 147–51

classroom environment
   bottom-up classrooms, 68–70
   and response to learning, 142–45
   top-down classrooms, 111–12
Clay, Marie, 135
Clinton administration education policy, 42
coaches, for scripted reading programs, 82–83
competition, forced, 57–61
comprehension
   and decodable text, 74
   impacts of phonics instruction on, 94–95
   integrating with skills instruction, 116–21, 124
   with Open Court Reading program, 88
   as outcome, in NRP meta-analysis, 92–93
   studying, in bottom-up classrooms, 70, 76–77
confidence, value of building, 126, 143
conflicts of interest, 10, 30, 72–73, 100–110. *See also specific individuals*
consultants, governmental, 30
context, and learning to read, 129–30
controlled vocabulary, 71–75
controls, in experimental research, 91–92
conversation, and learning to read, 124–25
cooperation, learning, 63–64, 111–12
core knowledge, determining, 40
corporation-run schools
   exemption from standardized testing, 21, 35, 37
   profit-making potential, 13–15, 23
   and school "reform," 13
   supplemental programs, 30
costs of reading programs, 81–83, 99. *See also* profit-making opportunities
criterion-referenced tests, 31–34
critical thinking, 14–15, 124–25
cueing systems, 134

"debilitating system," as buzzword, 25
decodable text, 71–74, 92
democracy. *See* citizen participation
demonstrating, modeling, 118, 123
developmental differences, and standardized testing, 35, 49
dialects, and phonics instruction, 130–31
DIBELS (oral fluency test), 107–8
Dick and Jane readers, 129

164

Direct Instruction (DISTAR) reading program (McGraw-Hill), 88, 104–5, 109
discouragement, and keeping silent, 3, 147
distribution, normal, 44
dropout rates, 52–53
Duckett, Peter, 132–33, 136
dyslexia cure, 138–41

Edison Schools, 13–14
education policy. *See* No Child Left Behind legislation; *Report of the National Reading Panel (NRP)*
effect size, in NRP meta-analysis, 93, 94–95
effective teaching, debates about, 67–68
effectiveness of government-mandated programs, 87–89
Ehri, Linnea, 104, 132
Einstein, Albert, 27, 56, 63, 110
English as a second language learners, 116–17, 129–30
English language, irregularity of, 127–28
errors, scoring, 37–39
essay questions, scoring of, 39–40
ethics, values, and corporate business model, 15, 59–61
excerpts, as reading materials, 76
experimental research. *See* research, scientific
the Expert, 4–6, 18–19, 30
eye movement research, 132–33

facts versus understanding, 66, 70–71
failure, fear of, impacts on learning, 51–52
false evidence. *See* research, scientific
fast reading, 135
federal control of schools, 7, 20–23, 34–35. *See also* No Child Left Behind legislation
findings from NRP report, misrepresentation of, 97–99
Finn, Chester, 11–14
fixations, 132
Florida school system, 44
fluency, 70, 132–34
followers, training children to be, 69, 142
Foorman, Barbara, 87, 101, 102
forced-out rates, 53–54
Fordham Foundation, 12, 15
fourth graders, developmental differences, 35
Fresno Bee, 86–87
Fuller, Ben, 11–17
funding, for NCLB legislation, 27, 28

government-approved programs, 45, 87–89. *See also* federal control of schools; No Child Left Behind legislation
graphophonemics, 134
Greene, Jane Fell, 103

Headlam, Alis, 138–41
"high standards," as buzzword, 12, 18, 29
Horn, Joe, 9
Houghton Mifflin reading programs, 81, 104
Houston, Texas, dropout rates, 53
humor, competitive, 58–59

Ignite educational software, 107
imposter syndrome, 6
independent reading, 136–38
individual rights, versus government mandates, 22
inference studies, 69, 76
information overload, and dependence on "experts," 3–4
"independent research," as buzzword, 18
"institute," as buzzword, 18
intimidation, 6–7, 34–35, 59–60, 84–85, 86–87
invented spelling, controversies about, 1, 113–16, 121–22

Jolly Phonics reading program, 88

Kame'enui, Edward J., 107–8
key words, 133
kindergarten, reading instruction, 112–15
Klein, Joel I., 54
Kohn, Alfie, 34
Krashen, Steve, 48, 138

labeling, ranking, and bullying, 60
Lagenberg, Donald, 104
Langer, Ellen, 127
Language! program (Sopris West), 19, 72–73, 89, 103–4, 122
learning disabled students, programs for, 139
learning mechanisms, 67–68
legitimate authority, 6–7
lessons, scripted, pacing of, 82–83
letter-by-letter reading, 132–33
literature supplements, 77–80
local control, 7, 22–25, 58, 82–83
low-level learning, NCLB emphasis on, 66, 124–25, 142
"low-performing" schools, 21, 34–35, 44
Lundberg, Ingvar, 102
Lyon, Reid, 20, 82

macromeaning (semantics), 134
margin of error, and standardized tests, 44
Martin, Bill Jr., 126
math, teaching of in bottom-up classrooms, 70
McGraw, Harold III, 104–5
McGraw, Harold, Jr., 105

McGraw-Hill Publishing
 Direct Instruction (DISTAR) program, 88,
  104–5, 109
 Language! program, 19, 72–73, 103
 Open Court Reading program, 19, 81–85,
  86–88
 Rod Paige's links with, 105–6
 use of Widmeyer-Baker public relations
  company, 99
McKay, Robert, 143–44
mean (average), 43
meaning-focused education, misconceptions
 about, 68, 115–16
medical (experimental) research model, 91
memorization, emphasis on, 70–71
meta-analysis, by NRP, 89–92, 95–96, 104
Moats, Louisa, 72–73, 89, 103–4, 113, 121–22
Month-by-Month Phonics (MM), 81–82
motivation, and failure, 52
MRI-based dyslexia studies, 139–41
multiple choice questions, 36–37

Nation's Report Card (U.S. Dept. of Educa-
 tion), 50
National Assessment of Education Proficiency
 (NEAP), 50
National Education Association (union), 12, 27
National Health and Human Development
 Agency, 72
National Institute of Child Health and Devel-
 opment (NICHD), 72–73, 89, 103, 139
National Reading Panel report. *See Report of the
 National Reading Panel*
National Reading Panel scientists, 100–110, 137
NCLB. *See* No Child Left Behind legislation
Nelson, Jim, 106–7
New York City education system, 37–39, 53–54,
 81–82
news stories, evaluating critically, 11–19
No Child Left Behind legislation
 and bottom-up teaching methods, 68
 contradictions in, 23
 funding for, 27
 impacts of, 19–20, 27, 37–39, 50–52
 importance of understanding, 10, 28, 42–43
 intimidating nature of, 81–82, 84–87
 Opportunity Scholarships, 25–26
 summary of contents, 20–22
nonsense stories, 74
nonsense words, ability to read, as NRP outcome, 92
norming (normalization) process, for standardized tests, 43–47
Nowakowski, Jerri (Voyager team member), 19

Office of Special Education, 139
Ohanian, Susan, 151

Open Court Reading program (McGraw-Hill).
 See also McGraw-Hill Publishing
 effectiveness of, 54, 84–88, 109
 intimidation tactics, 84–87
 involvement of Foorman and Adams in,
  102
 mandates for, 50, 81
 publicizing of, 19, 99
 scripted approach, 82
Opportunity Scholarships, 25–26
oral reading, as outcome, in NRP meta-analysis,
 92
Orton-Gillingham reading program, 88

PA. *See* phonics instruction, phonemic awareness (PA)
pacing of scripted lessons, 82–83
Paige, Rod, 25–26, 45, 53, 105–6
parents, intimidation of, 2–3, 6. *See also* local
 control
*Phonemic Awareness in Young Children: A Class-
 room Curriculum,* 103
phonics instruction, phonemic awareness (PA)
 accents and dialects, 129–31
 in bottom-up classrooms, 46–48, 71–75
 as buzzword, 1
 and comprehension, 94–95
 for dyslexic students, 138–41
 NRP-evaluated research about, 91–92, 94–
  95
 profit-making potential, 48–49
 role of, in learning to read, 126–29
 in top-down classrooms, 118, 119, 125–28,
  131–32
policy, education. *See* No Child Left Behind legislation
political involvement, 65
portfolio assessment, 31–32
practicing, and learning to read, 136
predictions, and comprehension, 123
preschool children, labeling of, 46–49
press releases, 18–19
Pressley, Michael, 87
private schools, exemption from standardized
 testing, 35, 37
professional development services, 83
profit-making opportunities
 literature supplements, 77–80
 professional development services, 30
 reading materials, worksheets and teaching
  manuals, 75–76
profit-making opportunities
 basal readers, 78–80
 consulting, 30
 phonics programs, 48–49
 standardized testing and scoring, 29–30, 38–
  40

prosody, 70
public education, impacts of NCLB legislation on, 12, 23, 26–27, 30, 37, 144
publicity, for reading programs, 18–19, 103–4
punctuation, teaching in top-down classrooms, 119
punitive approach to learning, 121

questions, on standardized tests, 41, 42

Ravitch, Diane, 15
Reading First grants, 21, 23–24, 30, 108
reading growth, NRP definition, 92
reading instruction
    authentic versus artificial approaches, 123–24
    controversies about, 67–68
    and eye movement research, 132–33
    government approved programs, 78–80, 89–90
    and importance of practice, 136
    phonics and basal readers, 71–72
    in top-down classrooms, 122–30
Reading Language Arts Framework for California, 107
Reading Mastery. *See* Direct Instruction reading program
reading materials
    abridged, artificial, 71, 75–76
    in top-down classrooms, 119, 138
Reading Recovery program, 45, 135–36
Reading Specialist credentials (Voyager program), 105–6
reading
    NRP definition, 95
    proficiency, and NCLB legislation, 50, 87–88
    relationship to writing, 124
"reform," as buzzword, 18
relaxation, importance of, 57
relevance, and learning, 127
reliability of standardized tests, 35–36
renorming, 46, 47
Report of the National Reading Panel (NRP)
    analytical shortcomings, 91–92
    background and purpose, 89
    comments on, by panel members, 98, 100
    dissemination of findings, versions, 90, 96–100
    on effectiveness of decodable text, 72–73
    methodology, 89–92, 104, 109
    outcome measures, 92–94
    recommended reading programs, 82, 89–90
    results, 87–90, 129–30
    use of, as buzzword, 18
Report of the Subgroups (NRP), 96
research, by NRP

design and analytical shortcomings, 95–99, 137–38
    focus on special needs students, 109
    meta-analysis methodology, 89–93, 104
    results of, 94–95
research, scientific
    as buzzword, 18
    on decodable text, 72–73
    on effectiveness of Open Court, 87–88
    evaluating accuracy of, 15–16
    on eye movement, 132–33
    on phonics, 91
    versus classroom-based research, 137–38
Resisting Reading Mandates (Garan), 84–85, 101
results, from standardized tests, 51
retaining children, 44, 52
ridicule, as media staple, 59–60

Sarason, Seymour, 22
SATs (Scholastic Aptitude Tests), 34–35, 50
school reform, 1, 10–11, 13
schools. *See also* bottom-up classrooms, methods; top-down classrooms, methods
    as artificial environments, 142
    federal control over, 7, 20–23, 34–35
    impact on children, 2
    intimidating nature of, 6–7
    time spent in, 143
science studies, in bottom-up classrooms, 70–71
scientifically proven methods
    as buzzword, 18
    and core reading programs, 81
    and the standardized test business, 44–45
scoring standardized tests, 39–40
scripted reading programs. 1, 82–86, 90
self-esteem, 51–52, 57, 72
semantics (macromeaning), 134
shallow thinking. *See* critical thinking
Shanahan, Timothy, 95–96
shared reading, 125–26
shared writing, 119
Shaywitz, Sally, 141
sight words, 129
Simmons, Deborah C., 107
simulators, effectiveness of, as teaching tool, 127
skills instruction, in top-down classrooms, 116–19, 125–28
skills-first instruction. *See* bottom-up classrooms, methods
social skills, importance of learning, 111–12
social studies, in bottom-up classrooms, 70–71
socialization, role of schools in, 143
Sony, falsification of movie reviews, 9–10
Sopris West, 89, 103, 122. *See also Language!* program
special education populations, NRP focus on, 108–9

speech-to-print correspondence, 126
spelling
    invented, controversies about, 1, 113–14
    as outcome, in NRP meta-analysis, 92
    and phonics instruction, 121–22
    teaching in top-down classrooms, 116–21
spin, as information, 5
standardized tests, testing
    child-to-child comparisons, 43
    effects of, 30, 34, 50–52
    essay questions, 39–40
    exemption of private schools from, 35, 37
    and federal funding, 34–35
    methodology, 43–44
    multiple choice questions, 36–37
    profit-making potential, 35, 38–39
    reliability, 33, 35–39
    secrecy about questions, rationale for, 42
    time lag for reporting results, 51
    validity, 36–37
    variability among standardized tests, 40–41
    versus criterion-referenced tests, 33–34
Stanford 9 (Harcourt), 44
statistical analysis
    by NRP, criticisms of, 95–96
    for standardized tests, 43–44
stress, and testing, 56–57, 61–64
Summary Booklet (NRP), 97–99
summer reading, 138
supplemental programs, 30
"Survey: Teachers See Selves as Scapegoats"
    (Finn), 11–17
"sweeping reform," as buzzword, 19
Sylvan Learning programs, 30, 44–45, 135
syntax, 134

teacher manuals, guides, 71, 75–76, 82–83
teacher-centered classrooms, 68–69
teachers
    absence from NRP, 137
    "bad," characterizations of, 12, 16
    changing role of, 66, 68, 74, 83
    intimidation of, 45, 84–87
    memorable, 145–46

opportunities for advocacy, activism, 7,
    149–50
teachers' unions, 12, 27, 149–50
test preparation, time spent on, 50–51, 66
testing. See also standardized tests, testing
    as buzzword, 1, 35
    DIBELS, 107–8
    fears about, 51–52
    stress associated with, 56–57
    testing models, 30–32
Texas, impacts of NLB policy in, 52–54
thinking, time for, 3–4
top-down classrooms, methods, 111–28, 144
Torgesen, Joseph, 18–19, 45, 107, 108
totalitarian countries, control of schools in, 23
traditional classrooms. See bottom-up class-
    rooms, methods
training, for scripted reading programs, 83
tutoring, government-subsidized, 21

U.S. Department of Education, 23, 50
unions. See teachers' unions

validity of standardized tests, 36–37
video summary of NRP report, 97
vocabulary, controlled, 71–72, 74–75
vouchers, 144
Voyager Learning program
    federal government support for, 106–7, 135
    imposition of on schools and teachers, 45
    publicity for, 18–19

West Baltimore, MD, Edison Schools, 14
Widmeyer-Baker public relations company, 99–
    101
Wizard of Oz metaphor, 5–6, 8
WOO (World of Opportunity), 150–51
word identification, as outcome, in NRP meta-
    analysis, 92
word-by-word reading, 132–33
worksheets, 76–77
writing instruction, 112–21, 124

Yatvin, Joanne, NRP minority report, 100